Pickle & Ferment

Pickle & Ferment

Preserve Your Produce
& Brew Delicious Probiotic Drinks

Susan Crowther & Julie Fallone

Foreword by Taylor Hill, ND

Skyhorse Publishing

Skyhorse Publishing books may be purchased in bulk at special discounts for sales promotion, corporate gifts, fund-raising, or educational purposes. Special editions can also be created to specifications. For details, contact the Special Sales Department, Skyhorse Publishing, 307 West 36th Street, 11th Floor, New York, NY 10018 or info@skyhorsepublishing.com.

Skyhorse® and Skyhorse Publishing® are registered trademarks of Skyhorse Publishing, Inc.®, a Delaware corporation.

Visit our website at www.skyhorsepublishing.com.

10 9 8 7 6 5 4 3 2 1

Names: Crowther, Susan, author. | Fallone, Julie, author. | Hill, Taylor, writer of foreword.
Title: Pickle & ferment : preserve your produce & brew delicious probiotic drinks / Susan Crowther & Julie Fallone ; foreword by Taylor Hill, ND.
Description: New York, NY : Skyhorse Publishing, [2023] | Includes bibliographical references and index. | Summary: "60 classic and unique recipes for probiotic-rich ferments such as sauerkraut, pickled veggies, salsas, kimchi, sourdough, jun tea, and more!"-- Provided by publisher.
Identifiers: LCCN 2023005728 (print) | LCCN 2023005729 (ebook) | ISBN 9781510775756 (Print) | ISBN 9781510777941 (Ebook)
Subjects: LCSH: Cooking (Fermented foods) | Fermented foods. | Canning and preserving. | Salting of food. | Bacteria--Health aspects. | Human body--Microbiology. | LCGFT: Cookbooks.
Classification: LCC TX827.5 .C76 2023 (print) | LCC TX827.5 (ebook) | DDC 664/.024--dc23/eng/20230301
LC record available at https://lccn.loc.gov/2023005728
LC ebook record available at https://lccn.loc.gov/2023005729

Cover design by Kai Texel
Cover photo by Julie Fallone
Interior design by Chris Schultz

Print ISBN: 978-1-5107-7575-6
Ebook ISBN: 978-1-5107-7794-1

Printed in China

Authors' notes:

My introduction to live fermentation came from a raw pickle workshop based on the book, *Wild Fermentation* by Sandor Ellix Katz, an unassuming man who is world-renowned as the Fermentation Guru. I was already familiar with fermentation, but a friend was interested in attending. So I figured I'd offer the favor of accompanying her.

That favor changed my life . . . and humbled me. As much as we may know about something, there is always room to learn more. At the time, I was writing my first book, *The No Recipe Cookbook* (Skyhorse, 2013). I was so inspired by Katz that I featured his Live Culture Sour Pickles as the one and only recipe in that book.

Since then, I've been live fermenting like a crazy person. No vegetable sees the compost bin until it's visited the pickle crock. Mason jars line all the counters and fruit scrap sodas fill the cupboards. Extra refrigerators crowd the basement. People roll their eyes (and sometimes hold their noses) when entering our house.

I can't help myself.

Once the live fermenting bug bites, you are hooked, fallen down the rabbit hole, gone for good. Live fermenting is like joining a really healthy cult. You surround yourself with kindred spirits—trillions of them, in fact—as you will soon see. These trillions of tiny friends do more to heal your mind, body, and spirit than any medicine I've ever encountered, and in the most delicious way.

I'd like to introduce you to my friends.

In good health, always,
Susan Crowther

Ask any great chef what the secret ingredient is in all their recipes and they will tell you the same thing: love. People are encouraged to talk to their plants because the carbon dioxide helps them grow. But with cooking, there's a bit more to it. It's as if the emotions you are feeling are ingredients in the creation you are making.

In this book, we explore a very particular type of cooking called live fermentation. Since living things are dynamic, we really want to keep that love alive! As you begin this journey, remember to invite joy and gratitude into your kitchen. Your veggies will appreciate it!

Julie Fallone

CONTENTS

Foreword by Taylor Hill, ND viii

Live Fermentation..1
    Health Benefits of Live Fermenting 5
    Raw Pickling and Lacto-Fermenting...9
    Mind-Gut Connection 10
    Myths of Fermentation 13

Basics of Live Fermenting and Raw Pickling..............................15
    The Methods: Dry Salt and Brine...18
    Tips and Troubleshooting..22
    Fermentation Checklist 25

The Recipes 27
    Veggies and Fruit...29
    Cultured Beverages...73
    Recipes Using Fermented Foods..107
    Fermented Body Care Products 153

Resources 158
    Sources 161
Metric Conversions 162
Index 163
About the Authors..169
About the Contributors..170
Acknowledgments...171

FOREWORD
BY TAYLOR HILL, ND

When I was asked to write the foreword to *Pickle & Ferment*, I was excited to be able to give my endorsement. As a naturopathic doctor and a fermenting enthusiast, I am well aware of the health benefits and longstanding traditions of fermentation. Susan Crowther makes an excellent guide on this journey. She has a wealth of knowledge and experience of cooking in general and fermenting in particular. You are in excellent hands using this book as a resource.

Susan has created a beautiful book that will be useful for all regardless of your experience level. Not only does she provide an excellent foundational knowledge and wonderful recipes, but the pictures throughout the book are vibrant and beautiful and will make you want to flip through the pages again and again.

If you're new to fermentation, this book will give you the knowledge necessary to begin fermenting with confidence. Solid template recipes have been provided as a jumping off point. If you've been fermenting for a while, there are many creative and unique recipes included that will hopefully inspire you in new ways.

Digestion is the foundation of all health. You could say that the digestive system is the soil out of which good health grows. Our digestive system is at the very core of our body and is directly or indirectly connected to all other systems. When it is impaired, it impacts the rest of the body in several ways:

First, digestion is how our body gets all its energy input and nutrients. When the digestive system isn't operating normally, we don't break down our food as well. This means that both the macronutrients and micronutrients aren't free to be absorbed the way they should be.

Second, when digestion isn't correctly working, several harmful substances can be produced. Improperly digested foods contribute to inflammation of the intestinal walls. This inflammation makes it easier for things to pass through the intestinal wall into the blood, creating a "leaky gut." When partially digested proteins pass into the bloodstream, they are more likely to trigger immune system reactions as an allergy or sensitivity.

Incompletely digested starches and sugars may feed yeast and opportunistic bacteria that can multiply out of check in this environment.

Third, the gut has been found to be connected to our brain and nervous system. This is called the gut-brain axis and has a strong impact on mental health, stress, memory, and mood including anxiety and depression. All these functions of the GI tract are dependent on a healthy gut microbiome.

I have also contributed several sidebars throughout the book that provide additional scientific and medical knowledge related to fermented foods. They will show that the evidence for the benefits of fermentation comes not only from the wisdom of our elders but has been reaffirmed by modern research. Fermented foods are one of the best things you can add to your daily diet.

May you enjoy this book and apply it to your life in good health!

LIVE FERMENTATION

*I couldn't believe that the answers I had been seeking . . . the wellness that I wanted for
my family . . . came to me . . . in the form of food.*

Donna Schwenk, *Cultured Food Life*

Fermenting, in the simplest definition, is changing food into a healthier version of itself—a
version that basically stays fresh, forever.

Sounds kind of magical, doesn't it?

It kind of is.

After cooking for over fifty years, fermenting is the most exciting, practical—and,
yes, magical—type of cooking I've ever encountered.

My friend, Donica (who you'll meet later), asked if I could sum up fermentation in
one neat little sentence. One book later, I'm still trying. It's hard to sum up magic. But
let's give it a shot.

Fermenting is what happens when you mix two things together: food and salt. (There
are other ways to ferment, but this book focuses on this particular method.)

As soon as food and salt are combined, they wake up microbes—bacteria and yeast
that are living in and on the food. You can actually see the microbes. They create the gray
fuzziness on the surfaces of fruit and veggies (like our cabbage on the left).

Now there are three things: food, salt, and microbes. The microbes are the magicians.
They:

1. Eat the food.
2. Create more microbes.
3. Change the food.

Fermentation is much more complicated and just as simple as that.

Fermentation could not happen without microbes, just as we could not exist without
microbes. Your body is not who you think it is. Did you know you are more microbe than
human? It's true. Over half the cells of the human body are actually bacteria, viruses, and

fungi, collectively known as the *microbiome*. About 40 trillion microbial cells exist in a human body, versus 30 trillion actual human cells. Collectively, these microbes weigh in at about three to four pounds, roughly the weight of your brain.

Most people think of bacteria as bad. We're accustomed to believing that we should live an antibacterial life. We use antibacterial soap. We take antibiotics. But in fact, many bacteria are not only good, they are required for our survival. Fermentation is the process that creates these healthy microbes.

"Ferment" comes from the Latin root *fervere,* "to boil." And fermenting foods *do* appear to be boiling. Good bacteria eat sugars and starches in foods. As they digest this fuel, they multiply quickly, creating by-products—gases and acids, which bubble. This is how we know fermentation is happening. Their bubbly feast transforms the food into something better, creating a more nutritious food with more complex flavors and pleasing textures. And the acids preserve and protect the food from spoiling. Magic.

Fermentation is an ancient food preserving technique that has been used for thousands of years. It allowed foods to be saved during the long winter months when fresh foods were unavailable. Most fermented products stay fresh for months, even years.

Like many culinary wonders, fermenting was probably discovered by accident. A common guess is that some nomad traveled across some desert carrying milk inside a canteen made from cow's stomach. Stomach linings contain a substance, rennet, which coagulates milk. So, while the nomad walked through the hot desert, the milk and rennet combined and then fermented. When he reached his destination, the milk had curdled and transformed into cheese—a most delicious discovery.

Fermenting creates a certain *something* to food that we naturally crave. Some of our favorite foods are fermented, like cheese, chocolate, coffee, wine, beer, soy sauce, and the condiment Tabasco. Any food can be fermented. And fermentation travels around the globe.

Every culture ferments. In Asia, common fermented foods include soy sauce, but also miso, tempeh, natto, and kimchi. Europe boasts sauerkraut, salami, prosciutto, mead, and cultured milk products like kefir, crème fraiche, and quark. The Americas have pickles, yogurt, chicha, hot sauce, hot peppers, horseradish, and kombucha.

Fermented foods are unique to each area due to the culinary phenomenon, *terroir*—the characteristic taste and flavor imparted to a food by the environment in which it is produced. *Terroir* creates unique microbes responsible for fermentation such as San Francisco's trademark sourdough bread. So not only does every place on earth ferment, but every ferment is different, based on where it lives.

This book explores a specific type of fermentation: raw pickling or live fermentation. Live-fermented foods are the healthiest to eat and easiest to make. Live fermentation is simpler than canning and the food lasts longer than freezing. This technique saves time and energy, as it cuts down on heating and cooking. Live-fermented foods do not require refrigeration. Plus, they can stay fresh indefinitely.

In addition to saving energy costs, fermenting increases a food's health benefits. Live-fermented foods are healthier than their original raw products. Vital nutrients and vitamins—often destroyed with heating—are not only kept alive, but improved. And other nutrients are actually created during fermentation.

If live-fermented foods are so great, why doesn't everyone eat them all the time? The simple answer is technological: we don't need to eat them anymore. With the advent of refrigeration, pasteurization, preservatives, and industrialized food preparation, fermentation went out of style, and even worse, gained a bad reputation. The truth about live fermentation is that it is one of the best and safest ways to prepare and preserve our food.

A census of all life on earth was completed in 2018. It was estimated that there are 550 gigatons of life on the planet. The largest share of that, about 82 percent, is plants (450 Gt) and about 13 percent is bacteria (70 Gt). All animals make up less than 0.5 percent, and humans only account for 0.01 percent (0.06 Gt) of all life on the planet. There are 1,166 times more bacteria than there are humans (by mass). (Bar-On, Phillips, & Milo, 2018)

HEALTH BENEFITS
OF LIVE FERMENTING

There are so many reasons to eat fermented foods, but the most important reason is that they are the fastest way to increase your health. We are learning more and more about the physiological effects of eating fermented foods and what those microbes are doing inside our bodies. They do a ton of stuff! Every year, more microbes are being discovered that are responsible for more and more body processes. With literally trillions of microbes in our bodies, there may be trillions of different processes happening. We may never know everything that the microbe kingdom does to regulate and improve our health.

Live-fermented foods (LFFs) belong to a category called *superfoods*—foods that are nutrient-packed with proteins, vitamins, minerals, water, enzymes, probiotics, and electrolytes. Superfoods are considered to be the most important for health and wellbeing.

LFFs are also classified as *functional* foods. Functional foods offer health benefits beyond their nutritional value. Fermentation actually *increases* vitamins and minerals in food, including the vitamin B spectrum—folic acid, riboflavin, niacin, thiamin, and biotin—and vitamin C, too. Plus, fermenting makes all nutrients easier to absorb, which means we get more bang for our food buck.

LFFs provide enzymes—protein chemicals needed for every bodily action and reaction. Enzymes help us to see, hear, move, think, and feel. Enzymes are needed to digest food.

Enzyme supplies decrease with age, so the best way to support our bodies is to eat food high in enzymes. Cooked food has no live enzymes, raw food has some, and fermented foods are abundant!

LFFs pre-digest our food. Microbes feed on sugars and starches, essentially breaking down the food before we even eat it; we're like the baby birds. Gluten is predigested in grains, and lactose is predigested in dairy (which is why gluten and lactose-intolerant people can often eat fermented foods that contain gluten and lactose). Fermented beans are predigested, and so we feel less gassy after eating them. Fermentation breaks down complex proteins into readily digestible amino acids. And because the bacteria are eating the sugars and starches, live-fermented foods contain less sugar and fewer calories than their raw counterparts.

LFFs don't just break down foods and create nutrients; they create life! Remember our friends, the microbes? LFFs are rich in probiotics, the helpful microbes living inside our guts. LFFs are also rich in *prebiotics*—fibers that feed probiotics. Live-fermented foods are *synbiotic*—containing both pre- and probiotic substances. This is a rare culinary treasure.

Not only are LFFs easily digestible, they actually improve the system itself. The "gut" is our entire gastrointestinal (GI) tract or digestive system—the highway from mouth to rear. Fermented foods heal the highway. In addition to digesting food, the gut is also where much of the immune system resides. A healthy gut, therefore, creates a healthy immune system, where natural antibiotic, anti-tumor, anti-viral, and anti-fungal substances are created right inside us. Fermented foods create acidic conditions, which help destroy pathogens (disease-causing bacteria).

In addition to creating good substances and environments, fermentation also fights for us. LFFs neutralize dangerous substances called *anti-nutrients*—in particular, phytates, found in grains, nuts, seeds, and legumes. Phytates bind to minerals and disrupt their absorption, leading to mineral deficiencies.

All this, plus, fermented foods taste delicious! LFFs have that *umami* flavor we crave. And by the way, it is not our bodies craving foods; it is our microbe kingdom. When we eat healthy foods, we grow healthy microbes, which crave healthy foods. We create symbiosis, a win-win relationship.

My mother always says when you visit someone's house, always leave it the same or better than you found it. Live-fermented foods don't just help us survive; they help us to *thrive*. (Mama would be proud.)

Phytic acid is often called an anti-nutrient. It is found in plant grains, legumes, nuts, and seeds. Its role is to preserve the nutrients in the seed or grain until it's been planted. When humans and animals consume foods with phytic acid, it prevents the absorption of minerals such as zinc, iron, and calcium. Fermentation has been shown to have the greatest decrease in the presence of phytic acid, up to 97 percent. By decreasing phytic acid, this makes those minerals more absorbable. This is a far greater reduction than can be achieved by soaking or sprouting. (Jianfen Liang, 2008)

RAW PICKLING AND LACTO-FERMENTING

Pickling is changing food with acid. Nowadays, when people think of pickles, they think of yellowish spears from the supermarket. Or they think of boiled canned veggies that gramma puts up every autumn. Or more recently, they think of "quick pickles" or "fast pickles" made by pouring hot sugared vinegar over cukes.

Raw pickles are none of these. The raw pickle is a different breed—the Real Deal. Raw pickles are actually live-fermented vegetables. The "pickle juice" is salt, water, and healthy microbes. No vinegar is added in raw pickling, as live fermenting produces its own natural vinegar. Raw pickles have a distinct pucker that cannot be replicated with cooked pickling methods.

Live fermentation is also called *lacto*-fermentation. Yeasts are commonly used for making alcohol (beer, wine, liquor). Alcohol fermentation is known as ethanol fermentation. Bacteria, on the other hand, are responsible for lacto-fermentation.

Lacto refers to a specific species of bacteria, *Lactobacillus* (first studied in milk ferments, hence, *lacto*). Lactobacillus is found in many foods and lives in and around plants, animals, and humans. It resides in our gastrointestinal tracts, lungs, skin, mouths, and other orifices. Lactobacillus bacteria convert sugars into lactic acid. Lactic acid is a natural preservative that inhibits the growth of harmful bacteria. It also increases vitamin and enzyme levels in the food and improves the digestibility of fermented food.

Live fermenting, raw pickling, lacto-fermenting . . . it can be confusing. For this book, a way to think about them is with methods. In live fermenting, veggies and salt are used in a method called "dry-salt." Raw pickling uses both salt and water, which is the "brine method." And both methods rely on Lactobacillus as their star quarterback. But, basically, it is all the same process: raw food is immersed in salty liquid and allowed to rest while the magic happens.

In 2017 an American study was performed looking at the types of bacteria found in sauerkraut during fermentation. It found that, within two days of fermentation, the large variety of naturally occurring bacteria was decreased dramatically. The salty, anaerobic environment favored the Lactobacillus so much that it went from a small percentage of bacteria to making up almost the entirety of bacteria found in the sauerkraut. (Zabat MA, 2018)

MIND-GUT CONNECTION

The microbiome kingdom functions as an extra organ in your body and plays a huge role in your health. There are at least 1,000 species of bacteria in the human gut, and each of them plays a different role in your body. In modern medicine, we've come to associate "bacteria" with "bad." While some bacteria are associated with disease, others are extremely important—necessary, in fact—for the immune system, heart, weight, and many other aspects of health.

As we've briefly discussed, the digestive system is responsible for much more than simply digesting food and making waste. Most of the immune system resides within the intestines. And incredibly, we've located a "second brain" located down there.

Ever had a gut feeling? Ever have a queasy stomach when you're nervous, like just before public speaking? Your brain and belly are intimately connected. Not only that, but they also affect each other's health: when we experience mental illness, our digestion also suffers; and when our digestion is hindered, we become mentally unwell.

This happens because of a complex communication system called the *gut-brain axis*—where electrical and chemical messages travel between the gut and brain. Neurons are cells found in the brain and central nervous system. They tell the body how to behave. There are approximately 100 billion neurons in the human brain. But the gut *also* contains neurons—about 500 million. These neurological signals communicate, traveling back and forth through a superhighway known as the vagus nerve.

Neurons communicate their messages through chemicals called neurotransmitters. Neurotransmitters control basically everything: thoughts, feelings, emotions, hormones, and body processes. One example is serotonin, the pleasure chemical. Serotonin contributes to feelings of happiness and also helps regulate our body clocks.

Neurotransmitters are produced mainly in the brain, but are also created by microbes residing in the gut. Remember those enzymes? They are responsible for creating neurotransmitters. About 95 percent of serotonin is produced in the gut. Gut microbes also produce a neurotransmitter commonly called GABA, which helps control feelings of fear and anxiety. When our microbe kingdom is imbalanced, these vital brain chemicals are, too.

The microbiome communicates with the immune system, controlling how the body responds to infection. The mind-gut connection also helps regulate inflammation. Gut microbes control what is passed into the body through membranes or "gut walls." Microbes are like bouncers; if goodness lives in the gut, then goodness is allowed to enter into the bloodstream.

Intestinal walls are damaged by processed and refined foods. Even some whole foods cause damage. Grains, beans, and legumes contain gluten and lectins—sticky substances that cling to and tear at the fragile membranes, causing holes or "leaky gut." Undigested foods, bacteria, and toxic chemicals can then enter into the bloodstream through these leaks, causing the immune system to react (think "bad bouncer at the door"). The immune system is set to respond to foreign bodies entering the bloodstream. When this continues (because we keep eating), we experience "chronic immune overreactions" commonly referred to as autoimmune diseases.

Basically, our immune systems are forced to keep up with our dietary drama, and eventually, the immune system breaks and begins to overreact. It cannot tell the difference

between food and pathogen. As the immune system overworks, it inflames the body to "kill the bad guys"; as a result, we suffer inflammatory diseases such as arthritis, MS, diabetes, and IBS/Crohn's disease.

The brain can also become inflamed. Disorders such as depression, dementia, and schizophrenia have been linked to chronic inflammation. Some studies suggest that autism and other spectrum disorders are associated with chronic mind-gut inflammation. There are over one hundred autoimmune diseases, and we are just beginning to learn about them.

What can we do? We can create healthy gut walls by pre-digesting these sticky substances, helping them break down into nutritional substances that enter the bloodstream easily. We invite healthy residents inside these walls to help us pre-digest these foods. We eat foods abundant in these healthy residents.

Remember the expression, "You are what you eat?" That applies here. The food you eat directly affects the health and diversity of your gut bacteria. Remember our probiotic friends. Bifidobacteria and Lactobacilli help repair intestinal walls and prevent leaky gut syndrome. These species also prevent disease-causing bacteria from sticking to intestinal walls. Probiotics can reduce symptoms of IBS and other intestinal diseases.

Probiotics that affect the brain are often referred to as "psychobiotics." Some probiotics have been shown to improve symptoms of stress, anxiety, and depression. Lactobacillus and Bifidobacteria have been shown to reduce symptoms of anxiety and depression in people with clinical depression.

When your mind and body are healthy, we produce chemicals to regulate all our processes. Think of your body as your own private pharmaceutical factory and distribution center. You produce every neurochemical that your doctor might prescribe, and the cost is astronomically lower. Compare the cost of cabbage to Celexa.

What is the best way to deliver psychobiotics to our immune system and gut-brain axis? How do we keep our gut highways healthy? You guessed it. The fastest, best way is through live fermentation.

MYTHS OF FERMENTATION

Fermenting is a paradox: it's the safest, and yet most feared method of cooking. It used to be a necessary part of everyday life. Blame the fear of fermenting on modern preservation techniques like pasteurization and refrigeration, for they eliminated any need to preserve naturally. Fermenting is now a lost art, relegated to the unknown and mysterious. These unknown mysteries lead to urban legends.

This section reviews some common myths and hopes to dispel any lingering fears.

MYTH #1: FERMENTED FOOD IS ROTTEN FOOD

Remember this: Raw milk sours; pasteurized milk rots.

The moment we pick a fruit or vegetable, it begins to decompose. When we cook foods, they decompose faster. But live fermentation actually halts and reverses this decomposing process. Fermented foods are "pre-digested," not rotten. And in fact, the fermenting process can preserve food indefinitely.

MYTH #2: BACTERIA ARE BAD

We live in an age where antibiotics are the "good guys" and bacteria are the "bad guys." The prefix *anti* means against or opposing, and *bios* is the Greek word for "life"; therefore, antibiotic literally means *life-killing*. Unfortunately, this is the case with antibiotics. While they do "kill the bad guys"—the harmful bacteria that cause serious illnesses—antibiotics also kill many "good guys"—beneficial bacteria that perform countless bodily processes. Antibiotics are like a neutron bomb, non-discriminating, equal-opportunity killers.

And as we now know, not all bacteria are bad. In fact, many bacteria are not only good, but are necessary for our survival. So when we kill all bacteria, we are, in a real sense, killing ourselves. Live-fermented foods, on the other hand, are life-giving. They reinstate the "neighborhoods" decimated by antibiotics. It's why doctors now recommend that patients eat yogurt and other probiotic-rich foods after taking antibiotics—to rebuild our bacterial communities.

MYTH #3: FERMENTATION IS EXACT SCIENCE

In the fermenting world, there are the two opposing camps: art vs. science. Some books are meticulous in every single detail of fermentation. Recipes read more like a high school lab report.

Unlike canned or vinegar methods of pickling, live fermentation is actually less "perfect science" and more "experimental art." There are basic methods and guidelines, but there is a lot of flexibility. Fermented foods are very forgiving, so there is room to learn and experiment.

MYTH #4: FERMENTATION NEEDS A STARTER

A "starter" or "inoculant" is leftover fermented product from a previous batch. Some fermented foods do require a starter, such as sourdough bread, kefir, and kombucha. But most live-fermented foods rely on only salt (and time) for transformation.

MYTH #5: FERMENTATION IS A FAD

It sure seems like a fad. Fermentation is exploding in popularity. There are now fermenting degrees offered in most agricultural colleges, with hipster breweries and pickle shops opening in every college town. But fermentation has been around for thousands of years in every culture on the planet. And again, some of our favorite foods are fermented: coffee, chocolate, pickles, cheese, yogurt, and soy sauce. Fermentation has always been part of how humans eat, and it always will be.

MYTH #6: FERMENTED FOODS ARE A LUXURY

Fermented foods may seem like an accessory condiment. But it's the opposite: fermented foods are *the* most important food to consume.

Live fermentation is the one cooking method that actually *increases* the health of the food product, compared with cooking, which destroys vital enzymes and vitamins. Fermented foods are healthier than even raw foods because fermenting "pre-digests" hard-to-breakdown proteins, carbohydrates, and other complicated substances. And while we can get some nutrients through supplements (vitamins, probiotics, etc.), the most complete and absorbable sources are always living whole food. Therefore, live-fermented foods should be part of every person's diet, and even better, consumed with every meal.

Remember, we are more microbiome than human. We've got 40 trillion microbes swimming around in our bodies, and they all need to be fed a healthy diet.

So, ferment already!

MEATS
& SWEETS

POULTRY,
EGGS, & DAIRY

FISH & SEAFOOD

FERMENTED FOODS

FRUIT & VEGGIES,
WHOLE GRAINS, NUTS OR SEEDS,
LEGUMES & BEANS, OLIVE OIL, & HERBS

BASICS OF LIVE FERMENTING AND RAW PICKLING

If you let raw food rest, it ferments. On the counter, in the fridge . . . doesn't matter. Microbes grow and multiply. The problem is, *everyone* grows—the bad and the good. Food eventually ferments, and it also spoils.

So fermenting tricks are used to encourage the good microbes to grow abundantly and inhibit the bad ones from growing at all. It's important to "control the narrative," so to speak. In order for healthy robust fermentation to take place, there are certain conditions required by the microbes. Fermenting is like "Goldilocks and the Three Bears"; all the elements need to be *just right*.

Even when everything is just right, every batch of live-fermented food is unique. Live fermentation is alive and dynamic, ever-changing. Everything in the environment affects the outcome: the raw product; mineral content of salt; quality of water; and length of time. Plus, there are external variables like geography and the season. Sauerkraut fermented in December will grow differently in wintery Canada than in Australia, where it's summertime. Subtle variations in temperature, bacteria existing on the vegetables, and exposure to air can yield very different results. Some people say the mood of the fermenter even affects the pickled product. (It's why we always cook with love.)

Still, there are some basic elements required in all live fermenting and raw pickling:

1. FOOD

The standard rule is, the better the food, the better the ferment. Choose fresh, locally-sourced, organic products. The fresher the product, the more good bacteria are still alive. Organic produce is best, because pesticides also destroy the good microbes, which can hinder fermentation and destroy the final outcome (similar to how antibiotics kill the good with the bad).

2. SALT

Salt serves many purposes in fermentation: it creates flavor and texture by acidifying veggies, keeping them crisp and crunchy. Salt retains vitamins and other nutrients, making healthy food even healthier. And it preserves. Salt inhibits the growth of negative bacteria, fungus, and molds. Sauerkraut can keep indefinitely. I've eaten batches that have been refrigerated for years!

Therefore, it is critical to use the right kind of salt. Unrefined sea salts are best. They contain trace minerals, which aid in the fermentation process and create a probiotic-rich product. Unrefined sea salts are also free of preservatives and added iodine. Never use iodized salts, as they lack minerals necessary for proper fermentation.

Some recommended brands are Celtic Sea Salt, Redmond's Real Salt, and Pink Himalayan Rock Salt (see page 159 in the "Resources" section for more information).

Note: Higher-quality salts take more time to dissolve in water, so be patient when making brine.

3. WATER

The same rule applies: the better the water, the better the ferment. All these recipes refer to using "good" water. Well water or natural artesian spring water are ideal, as they also contain trace minerals which aid in fermentation. They are also free of fluoride and other added chemicals. Avoid tap water, which has chlorine. Chlorine kills bacteria and stops fermentation. If you must use tap water, filter it. At the very least, allow tap water to sit out uncovered, overnight, to evaporate some chlorine.

4. TEMPERATURE

For the healthiest batches, fermenting at room temperature is best—about 70 to 75 degrees Fahrenheit. After fermenting, ideal storage temperature is around 40 degrees Fahrenheit.

Fermentation naturally occurs in all temperatures. The warmer the room temperature, the faster your kraut will ferment. But faster isn't better. "Faster" can cause bacterial imbalances. Colder fermentation (in the refrigerator) stalls the growth of probiotics and nutrients.

5. TIME

Fermentation requires time—days, weeks, even months or years—and is never officially completed. Live-fermented product is never "done," but rather, transferred from room temperature to cold storage. Fermentation continues in cold storage, but at a much slower pace.

6. STARTERS

A "starter" is a probiotic-rich substance added to raw foods to initiate the fermentation process. Some include active dried yeast, raw vinegars, sourdough, and whey (liquid by-product of cheese-making). Another common starter is to use the fermented liquid from a previous batch. Think of them as "kick-starters," helping good bacteria to quickly take over.

Most of the recipes in this book do not need starters; instead, they rely on wild microbes that live on the food and in the environment all around us. This type of process is known as "wild fermentation." A few recipes do use starters; Jun Tea, for instance, uses a SCOBY (described later in that section). Starters can be added to any recipe to help get things going. But for most of these recipes, wild fermentation will do just fine.

THE METHODS: DRY SALT AND BRINE

There are two main methods: dry salt and brine. The *dry salt* method adds salt directly to vegetables. Veggies are chopped or shredded, exposing ample surface area for the salt to draw their natural moisture out.

The *brine* method adds both salt and water to the vegetables. Brining is used when the food product lacks its own natural juices and needs a bit of "juice boosting." Brining is also good for fermenting vegetables that you want to keep whole or in larger pieces.

Here are general outlines for both methods. Next we'll be applying these methods to the recipes.

1. CHOOSE INGREDIENTS

Yes, it's true . . . the fresher the ingredients, the better the final product. But fermenting is also about utilizing—utilizing bumper crops and produce that may be going soft. Fresh, not-so-fresh . . . they're both fine.

Whenever possible, use organic ingredients. Conventional produce is sprayed, and these pesticides and herbicides destroy the fragile microbiome needed for fermentation. Organic means *alive*.

Salt

A good ratio of salt to vegetables is about 2 percent by weight. Recipes range from 1 to 5 percent, so personal taste helps: veggies should taste salty but not *too* salty. It's best to stay in this range, for safety and flavor. Too little salt may allow the mold and bad bacteria to flourish and make mushy veggies. Too much salt may slow or even stop the fermentation process.

Percentages are clunky, so use the general rule of thumb:

DRY SALT method: 1 tablespoon of salt + 2 pounds of veggies.

BRINE method: 1 tablespoon salt + quart of water.

"DRY SALT" RATIOS: per 2 pounds of veggies

SALT VOLUME	PERCENTAGE
1 Tablespoon	2%
1½ Tablespoons	3%
2 Tablespoons	4%
3 Tablespoons	5%

"BRINE" RATIOS: per 1 quart of water

SALT VOLUME	PERCENTAGE
1 Tablespoon	2%
1½ Tablespoons	3%
2 Tablespoons	4%
3 Tablespoons	5%

2. ADD SALT

Dry Salt Method

In the dry salt method, salt is added directly to vegetables and fruits. Dry salt is used for produce that has a high water content, like cabbage in sauerkraut. The produce is shredded or finely chopped to allow its own natural juices to release. Salt is sprinkled onto the shredded produce, and then everything is kneaded together to release the natural juices. This encourages the good bacteria growth, which starts the fermentation process.

Brine Method

When fermenting larger pieces of produce—whole cucumbers or carrot sticks, for example—we use the brine method. Brine is simply salt dissolved in water. Water needs to be the correct temperature: too warm, and the lacto-bacteria die off; too cold, and the salt remains un-dissolved. Room temperature to body temperature is a good range. Remember, the water, like the food and salt, needs to be good quality, sourced from a well, spring, or filtered.

3. SUBMERGE INGREDIENTS

Live fermenting requires an *anaerobic*, or "without oxygen," environment. Anaerobic conditions encourage good bacteria to grow vigorously and prevent the bad bacteria from growing. To create this anaerobic environment, food must stay submerged underneath the brine and natural juices, protecting the food from oxygen exposure.

Glass, ceramic, or silicone fermentation weights keep cabbage submerged under the brine and natural juices. Substitutes for fermentation weights include:

- Cabbage and other large outer layers
- Large vegetable leaves
- Crosscut slices of veggies
- Ziploc bag filled with water
- Extra brine

4. SEAL, COVER, AND PLATE

Fermentation lids are game changers! They keep the good bacteria thriving and prevent bad bacteria and molds. Yes, you can ferment without fermentation lids: cover jars with cheesecloth, beeswax wrap, or a loosened Mason jar lid. But fermentation lids are pretty foolproof, so I use them every time. These lids keep live fermenting fun, not frustrating!

For further protection against oxygen, bacteria, and bigger critters (flies and bugs), cover sealed jars with natural cloths. A "natural" cloth is one made from natural fibers such as cotton, hemp, or linen/flax. Beeswax wrap also makes a great cover, as it contains natural antibiotic qualities that prevent bad bacterial growth (while protecting the good bacteria).

And lastly, it can be helpful to place the jars on a plate in order to catch any liquid overflow that may happen once fermentation gets going.

5. LEAVE THEM BE

Fermentation takes time. Those tiny critters need privacy to work their magic, so leave them alone. Fermentation is a spectrum; there is no correct day when it is "ready"; however, recipes suggest time ranges based on general taste preferences. If you're new to fermenting, stay on the earlier range, with just a few days. If you are a diehard, you may prefer to go longer for funkier flavor. While there are health benefits to longer fermentation, texture may suffer and veggies could become mushy; so leave them alone but check them often.

6. STOP AND GROW COLD

At some point, we stop the fermentation process: remove the fermentation lid; replace it with a regular jar lid; and store the product in the refrigerator. But this doesn't stop fermentation. Live fermenting is forever—meaning, it keeps going, indefinitely. Think about 7-year-old cheeses, 30-year-old miso, 100-year-old wines, or the infamous 1,000-year-old eggs . . . the fermenting process is simply controlled based on personal taste. So we don't actually "stop" fermenting; we transfer our ferments from warm environments to cold storage. This is known as "cold fermentation."

Cold fermentation is a good time to adjust a fermented product: add more salt or water to increase or decrease the saltiness; add more spices if it tastes bland. Then place the fermented product in the refrigerator and enjoy for days, weeks, or longer, while it continues to transform.

Table salt has been refined and iodide has been added to it. Iodide is in salt because people who used to live far from the ocean didn't eat seafood and therefore did not get enough iodine for their thyroid gland to function properly. Unfortunately, iodine is also antiseptic and can prevent growth in your ferment.

There are several varieties of sea salt. Sea salt is typically unrefined and comes in a variety of brands and types. It contains trace elements such as sulfate, magnesium, calcium, and potassium. Based on how they are produced, the mineral content will vary with a gray sea salt containing more minerals than a fleur de sel.

Himalayan pink salt is primarily mined in Pakistan. It is the result of a prehistoric ocean that was buried under lava from a volcanic eruption. This salt does contain trace amounts of a larger variety of minerals. The pink color is a result of these minerals: calcium, magnesium, potassium, copper, and especially iron.

TIPS AND TROUBLESHOOTING

SANITIZE VS. STERILIZE

Clean all counters, equipment, and utensils. It's not necessary to sterilize for live fermentation, but *sanitizing* does reduce exposure to random bad bacteria. Use diluted bleach or hydrogen peroxide in a spray bottle, rinse in hot water, and dry. And remember, we are encouraging bacterial growth, so never use antibacterial soap when cleaning. Also, never clean with scented soaps or detergents. No one wants Febreze-flavored pickles!

LEAVE SKINS ON

As a general rule, always leave skins on the produce. Microbes live on and in the skins of fruits and veggies. Furthermore, most of the nutrients also live within the skin. Gently wash the outer layer with water, and you're good to go. An exception would be produce with thicker skins, such as beets. But these, too, could be peeled after the fermentation process.

USE RIGHT AWAY OR KEEP COLD

Ideally, it's best to ferment as soon as the produce is harvested. But if that's not possible, keep produce cold until fermenting. All bacteria are lying dormant while the plant is growing. But once the plant is harvested, microbes grow on any place the plant is cut, damaged, or bruised. Keeping produce cold inhibits all growth until you're ready to ferment.

USE NON-REACTIVE EQUIPMENT

Glass, ceramic, or stainless steel are "non-reactive" materials. Ever drink orange juice from an aluminum bottle? Or wrap lasagna in tin foil? The acids in these foods react to certain metals. Non-reactive materials are safe for the acidic environment that fermenting causes.

MASON JARS

Most of these recipes use wide mouth Mason jars, as they are simple to use and fit the fermentation lids. But Mason jars are not required for fermenting. Other glass jars work well, such as jars with wire bale lids. Ceramic crocks are commonly used, too, but they allow more exposure to air. If using ceramic crocks, check ferments frequently.

FILL THE JAR AND LEAVE A SPACE

Lactic acid bacteria—the magical microbiome that produces sauerkraut—thrive in an oxygen-free environment. It's why we fill the jar closely to the top—to keep good bacteria in and oxygen out. But as the kraut ferments, the bacteria produce carbon dioxide or "off-gas." The off-gas builds up pressure in the jar. Your fermentation lids have "one way valves"—letting off-gas out while keeping oxygen from coming in. Most recipes recommend filling the jar up to an inch from the top, leaving just a bit of headspace for off-gassing.

IS IT READY?

Remember, there's no exact date when ferments are ready; it's up to your taste preference. But in general, fermentation takes 1 to 3 weeks.

Use all your senses to tell when your product is ready.

- Smell: "weird" but good—tangy, vinegary, yet fresh and vibrant
- Sight: slight change in color with tiny bubbles appearing throughout, effervescent
- Taste: sour and tangy, in a pleasing way. Texture is crunchy, with a "bite-back"—like *al dente* or a "par-boiled" texture.
- Touch: soft but still firm; rubbery and yielding
- Sound: liquid is fizzing with the quietest hissing (although rare to actually hear), and produce is squeaky when touched

CLOUDY BRINE

Cloudy brine is *good*! It is a natural by-product of a healthy fermentation process. Cloudy brine is a combination of lactic acid and yeast (and is the reason why live fermentation is also called lacto-fermentation). Lactobacillus bacteria convert sugar into lactic acid. Lactic acid prevents the growth of harmful bacteria. Over time the cloudiness can settle out of the brine to the bottom of the jar. Some batches are naturally cloudier than others, but all are safe to consume and taste delicious. Cloudy brine is a sign that you have a safe and successful ferment.

WHITE FILM = KAHM

Kahm is different than cloudy brine. Kahm is a thin white layer that completely covers the top of a fermented product. There may also be some small bubbles underneath this white layer. It may also present as white flakes along the surface. Kahm is edible wild yeast, neither good nor bad, and is common in live fermentation. Some people prefer to skim it off, but once Kahm presents in a fermented food, it grows back. It's best to consume the jar quickly; otherwise, Kahm will overtake the jar's environment.

BE CAREFUL!

When making fermented beverages, proceed with caution! Fermented beverages typically call for some sweetener to feed the yeasts. As microbes eat the sugar, they release carbon dioxide, which carbonates the beverage. If too much sugar is added or fermentation goes too long, the bottles may produce a lot of fizzing when opening. In rare cases, they may even explode. It's a good idea to ferment natural sodas in a cardboard box, garage, or basement. In general: USE CAUTION WHEN OPENING!

UTILIZE!

When you finish your kraut, drink the sauerkraut juice! It is rich in probiotics and enzymes. Enjoy it like a "gut shot" before a meal. Or use it as a "starter" for next batches to kick-start future ferments.

IS IT OKAY?

For various reasons—unclean equipment, old produce, not enough salt, too much oxygen, even dirty hands—mold may appear. Mold is different than cloudy brine or Kahm yeast. It can be toxic and should never be eaten. It's important to KNOW YOUR MOLDS!

- Mold is fuzzy and colorful: red, pink, green, black, and white.
- Mold smells funky and skanky, putrid and foul: think, "really dirty sock."
- Moldy fermented food becomes slimy. The brine is flat and lifeless.

If there is any mold, DISCARD THE BATCH AND BLEACH THE CONTAINERS. NEVER TASTE MOLD OR MOLDY FERMENTS!

And then, as in all of life, in a humble posture . . . start again! xo

FERMENTATION CHECKLIST

A checklist is *mise en place,* French for "everything in its place." Before fermenting, it's important to gather everything together—equipment, utensils, and food products—so that the process goes smoothly, stays sanitary, and remains fun!

Use this checklist in preparation for your fermenting session, in the order listed. First things first: first we prepare ourselves, then our kitchen, and then the supplies.

And at last, we prepare our product.

Name of Product:

Fermenting start date:

Fermenting end date (transferred to refrigerator):

Checklist:

- ☐ I am sanitary and prepared:
    - ☐ Hands washed
    - ☐ Clean apron
    - ☐ Clean hand towels
    - ☐ Counters are cleared off
    - ☐ Counters are washed and bleached
    - ☐ Kitchen is tidy and sanitary
    - ☐ Recipe selected
- ☐ All supplies are gathered:
    - ☐ Bleach/water spray bottle
    - ☐ Mason jar(s) or other containers
    - ☐ Fermenting lid(s)
    - ☐ Fermenting weight(s)
    - ☐ Kraut pounder and/or wooden spoon
    - ☐ Non-reactive bowls—glass, ceramic, or stainless steel
    - ☐ Beeswax wrap or natural cloth(s)
- ☐ All supplies are washed and bleached
- ☐ All ingredients gathered and rinsed (in warm water only)
- ☐ Starters/inoculators, if using
- ☐ Water prepared (filtered if using tap)
- ☐ Added ingredients or flavorings gathered
- ☐ Cup of tea poured to enjoy as you work!

THE RECIPES

VEGGIES AND FRUIT

Since sauerkraut and cucumber pickles are the most recognizable live-fermented products, they are described in more detail. Sauerkraut is generally made through the DRY SALT method. Raw Pickles use the BRINE method. These serve as templates for most recipes in the book.

Most recipes make one quart. Since sauerkraut and pickles are enjoyed more frequently, their recipes make two quarts.

For aesthetic purposes, the photographs show fermented products in a variety of containers. Some containers may not be the actual fermenting vessel.

BASIC DRY SALT RECIPE: LIVE-FERMENTED SAUERKRAUT

Sauerkraut is the flagship of all live-fermented foods. The basic ingredients are simple: cabbage and salt. Sauerkraut promotes healthy heart and blood, stronger bones, and weight loss. It's the salty fountain of youth. Sauerkraut is tangy, crunchy, zippy, and healthy, and it lasts forever! I've enjoyed batches after years of refrigeration. Like all ferments, the variations are endless, depending on personal taste and what is in the garden. Suggestions are listed at the end of the recipe.

MAKES: 2 QUARTS

INGREDIENTS:

2 heads of cabbage (about 4 pounds)

2 tablespoons finely ground sea salt

Materials:

2 wide mouth quart Mason or wire bale jars

Wooden spoon or kraut pounder

2 fermentation weights

2 fermentation lids

2 wide mouth stainless steel Mason jar lids

Covering cloth of organic material—cotton, linen, hemp, or beeswax wrap

1. Remove a few outer cabbage leaves and set aside. Thinly shred the remaining cabbage and place into a bowl.

2. Sprinkle most of the salt onto cabbage. Stir until cabbage begins to "sweat" and juice forms. Knead the sauerkraut, mashing it with your hands for several minutes. More juice will form. Taste the mixture. Add a bit more salt if desired—up to 3 tablespoons.

3. Transfer the kraut into a wide mouth Mason jar, about a cup at a time. Press the vegetables down with force, using a Kraut pounder or wooden spoon. Keep adding kraut, pressing firmly into the jar, until the juice rises up over the vegetables. If necessary, add a bit of water or "starter liquid" from a previous batch to completely cover the cabbage mixture.

4. Fill the jar about an inch to the top, leaving a little space for carbon dioxide formation or "off-gassing." Submerge the new sauerkraut with a fermentation weight. OR: Cover the kraut with a clean outer cabbage leaf. Immerse the leaf under the juice.

5. Seal the jar with a fermenting lid. Cover the jar with a natural cloth and store in a dark spot at room temperature.

6. Ferment the kraut at room temperature for two weeks, depending on the season (longer for winter, shorter for summer). Burp the kraut daily to release the gas produced during fermentation: open the fermentation lid or use a fermentation pump. Examine the kraut. It should smell fresh and tangy. The color will begin to change, as the kraut

becomes translucent. You will notice small bubbles. Keep pushing the kraut down below the liquid and secure the weight (or cabbage leaf) below the liquid, too. Reseal with the fermentation lid. You decide when to stop the official fermenting process, based on your own personal texture and flavor preferences. Generally, 2 to 3 weeks is standard.

7. Once the sauerkraut is ready to your liking, replace the fermenting lid with a stainless steel lid and transfer to the refrigerator or cold storage. The sauerkraut's flavor will continue to develop as it cold-ferments. Sauerkraut may last for month or even years.

VARIATIONS:

Combine with chopped, shredded, or finely sliced vegetables and fruits:
- Turnips
- Carrots
- Radishes
- Beets
- Apples
- Onions/Leeks
- Garlic
- Horseradish
- Peppers/Hot peppers

Add one or several seasonings:
- Caraway seeds
- Juniper berries
- Chili peppers
- Ginger root
- Turmeric
- Fresh herbs: Dill, Parsley, Arugula, Cilantro, etc.

Note: This is a dry salt recipe template for any fruit or vegetable. Dry salt method relies on products with their own natural juices instead of adding brine. In this method, the produce is shredded, finely diced, or minced, which helps draw out the natural juices. Fruit is easily dry-salted due to its high moisture content. Because dry salt product is shredded or finely chopped, the textures are softer and chewier than brine's crunchy counterparts.

BASIC BRINE RECIPE: RAW PICKLES

Pickles! The word makes everyone smile.

The word pickle originates from the Dutch word "pekel," meaning brine. Dutch farmers introduced pickles in New York City back in the seventeenth century. They grew cucumbers in Brooklyn, then brined and sold them in Lower East Side markets.

Raw Pickles are different from store-bought kinds. They are brighter green and sour, with a refreshing pucker. "Half sours" ferment for a shorter time than "full sours." It's up to personal flavor preference.

MAKES: 2 QUARTS

INGREDIENTS:

10 large edible plant leaves: grape, oak, horseradish, chard, etc.

4 pounds of cucumbers—about 15 pickling cucumbers

2 tablespoons finely ground sea salt

1 quart good water: well, spring, or filtered

1 large bulb garlic cloves

2 large heads of fresh dill OR 2 handfuls of fresh dill leaves, divided

Spices to taste: black peppercorns, red pepper flakes, mustard seeds, fresh horseradish root, etc.

Materials:

2 wide mouth quart Mason jars

2 fermentation weights

2 fermentation lids

2 wide mouth stainless steel Mason lids

Covering cloth of organic material—cotton, linen, hemp, or beeswax wrap

1. Gather a few large leaves (see recipe). Brush the leaves clean, but don't wash them.

2. Add the salt to the water and stir until the salt dissolves. Set aside.

3. Peel the garlic cloves.

4. Add a couple of the leaves, a few cloves of garlic, half the dill, and spices to the bottom of the jars.

5. Pack the cucumbers tightly on top of the spices. The longest ones work best at the bottom, smaller in the middle. Slice some lengthwise if necessary to fit in the jar. Leave 1 inch of space from the top of the jar. Place the remaining dill on top of the pickles. Pour the brine over the pickles.

6. Place a fermentation weight on top to keep the cucumbers under the liquid. OR: Place a few final leaves on top of the pickles as a weight covering. Immerse the weight/leaves under the brine. Seal the jar with a fermenting lid. Cover jar with a natural cloth and store in a dark spot at room temperature.

7. Ferment the pickles at room temperature for about one week, depending on the season (longer for winter, shorter for summer, etc.). Check the pickles daily—open the jar and examine them. They should smell

fresh and tangy. Their color will begin to change from bright green to a lighter green. Longer-fermented pickles will turn a yellow-grayish hue. The brine should turn cloudy with tiny bubbles. The brine will begin to taste fizzy and zingy. The pickles will begin to taste sour and crunchy. You decide when to stop the official fermenting process, based on your own personal texture and flavor preferences. Generally, 4 to 10 days is standard.

8. Once the pickles are ready to your liking, replace the fermenting lid with a stainless steel lid and transfer to the refrigerator or cold storage. The pickles' flavor and texture develops as it cold-ferments. Pickles are best eaten within a few months.

Optional salt ratios:

- 2 Tablespoons = Half Sour (bright, green & crunchy)
- 2.5 Tablespoons = Medium Sour (darker & saltier)
- 3 Tablespoons = Full Sour (intense pucker)

Note: This is a brine recipe template for any vegetable. The brine method uses larger cuts that pickle veggies while suspended in the salty brew. Larger cuts help retain the veggie's crunch and snappy texture.

Note: Save the leftover brine to drink or use as a starter in future ferment projects.

LIVE-FERMENTED ONIONS

Most people pickle onions with the "quick" method: heat vinegar, sugar, and spices, and then pour the hot sweet brine over the onions. Live fermenting onions keeps their valuable enzymes alive. Their flavor is unique and exquisite, with just the right sweet tang. Use them as the perfect condiment: on sandwiches and tacos, in soups and salads—everywhere, on everything. They are just soft enough and just crunchy enough, with a soft bite that gently bites back.

MAKES: 1 QUART

INGREDIENTS:

3 large onions

1–2 tablespoons finely ground sea salt

1. Cut the onions into thin slices or small pieces. Place in a bowl.

2. Sprinkle 1 tablespoon of salt onto onions and gently stir. Taste the mixture. Add a bit more salt if desired. Stir or toss by hand for a several minutes, until the onions begin to sweat and release their natural juices.

3. Press the onions into a wide mouth mason jar, about 1 cup at a time, using a wooden spoon or kraut pounder. Press firmly into the jar until the onion juice rises up and over the vegetables. If necessary, add a bit of water to submerge the onions.

4. Fill the jar about an inch from the top. Place a glass fermenting weight on the onions and press down further. The liquid should rise up or cover the weight. Seal the mixture with a fermentation lid. Cover the jar with a natural cloth and store in a dark spot at room temperature.

5. Leave the jars to ferment for 3 to 4 weeks. Check every day or so, to make sure things are brewing nicely. Open the lid and smell the onions. They should smell tangy and sour. Push the weight down to keep the onions submerged below the weight.

6. When ready, remove the fermentation weight and replace the fermenting lid with a stainless steel lid. Store in a refrigerator. Will keep nicely for about a year.

Note: After a year, live-fermented onions are still fine to eat, but may become a bit softer and taste more fermented, with a slight wine fragrance. One way to use them at this point is to puree them and then add to salad dressings, dips, sandwich spreads, onion sauce, etc.

LIVE-FERMENTED CARROTS

Most nutrients and healthy bacteria are just beneath the skin of plants, so leave those carrot skins on. Most recipes pickle carrot sticks; by shredding them, they keep their crunch and develop a fuller fermented, sweet-tangy flavor.

MAKES: 1 QUART

INGREDIENTS:

Two pounds carrots—garden or local carrots are best

1 tablespoon finely ground sea salt

Optional:

2 teaspoons fresh ginger root

1 cinnamon stick and 3 whole cloves or allspice

1. Gently hand-wash the carrots with water only. Shred carrots into a big bowl.

2. If using ginger root: scrub or gently peel the skin, and finely mince the ginger.

3. Add the sea salt (and optional spices, if using) to the shredded carrots. Mix well for several minutes with a wooden spoon or squeeze by hand. This releases the natural carrot juice and begins the fermentation process.

4. If using cinnamon stick and whole spices, place these at the bottom of a quart Mason jar.

5. Using a wide mouth funnel, transfer about a cup of the mixture into the jar. Pound down the mixture using a kraut pounder or wooden spoon. Add more mixture—about a cup—and pound down again. You will begin to see some juices rising to the top as you pound. Repeat this process until all the mixture is in the jar and firmly pounded down, leaving about an inch of space near the top.

6. Cover the mixture with a glass fermentation weight. Seal the mixture with a fermentation lid. Cover the jar with a natural cloth and store in a dark spot at room temperature.

7. Leave the jars to ferment for 3 to 4 weeks. Check every day or so to make sure things are brewing nicely. Open the lid and smell the carrots. They should smell sweet and tangy. Push the weight down to keep the carrots submerged below the weight.

8. When ready, remove the fermentation weight and replace the fermenting lid with a stainless steel lid. Store in the refrigerator.

Note: Carrots contain a high amount of sugar, which may begin converting to alcohol. Fermenting a quart at a time and then transferring to the refrigerator prevents this.

Another way to reduce the alcohol formation is to combine the carrots with a low-sugar vegetable such as turnips or cabbage.

RAW PICKLED GARLIC

Garlic adds pungent commanding flavor, especially raw. But sometimes that heat is a bit too much for some folks. Raw pickling is one way to enjoy garlic with all the enzymes and nutrients intact (raw) but without all the heat and intensity. The lacto-fermentation mellows it to a cross between raw and roasted garlic.

Some folks prefer to ferment garlic in whole cloves, but pureed garlic saves a step because it's minced and ready to go. Use it in everything!

MAKES: 1 QUART

INGREDIENTS:

12 bulbs of garlic (BULBS, not cloves!)

1 pint good water: well, spring, or filtered

2 teaspoons finely ground sea salt

1. Add the salt to the water and stir well until the salt dissolves.

2. Break the bulbs apart and peel the individual garlic cloves, removing any icky parts.

3. Puree the garlic cloves and brine into an easily pourable paste. Add more brine if necessary.

4. Pour the pureed garlic/brine mixture into a wide mouth quart Mason jar. Fill about an inch from the top.

5. Seal with a fermenting lid. Cover the jar with a natural cloth and store in a dark spot at room temperature.

6. Leave the jars to ferment for 3 to 4 weeks. Garlic is naturally anti-microbial, so generally ferments easily without any issues—no need to open the lid and check daily. Checking every few days is fine.

7. After a few weeks, replace the fermenting lid with a stainless steel lid. Store in a refrigerator. Keeps well indefinitely.

Note: Garlic stays well for a long time . . . years, even. The longer the garlic sits in cold storage the more delicious and nutritious it gets. As pickled garlic ages, it transforms into a beautiful blue-green hue. It's fine!

Optional:

Whole cloves: If you prefer whole garlic cloves, then add the cloves and brine directly into your Mason jar and follow instructions.

Garlic Scapes: Use garlic scapes instead of cloves. Cut up the scapes into small pieces—about 1-inch long—and then follow the same instructions, above.

RAW PICKLED PEPPERS

Peppers are another commonly canned veggie made healthier with live fermentation. The lactic acid in fermented hot peppers develops a tangy sweet flavor that balances the heat. Some recipes recommend removing the seeds to reduce heat, but utilizing the whole pepper boosts nutrition. Raw pickling is a pepper's best friend, retaining the spice while mellowing the burning heat. This recipe uses jalapeños, but try any hot peppers or combine several together. Also of note: this recipe calls for a whole lime, so make sure it—like all the produce—is organic.

MAKES: 1 QUART

INGREDIENTS:

2 pounds jalapeño peppers

1 tablespoon finely ground sea salt

1 pint good water: well, spring, or filtered

Optional:

1 organic lime and several garlic cloves

1. Add the salt to the water and stir until the salt dissolves. Set aside.

2. Remove the pepper stems and slice in crosscuts (circles). If using the optional ingredients, slice lime in crosscuts and peel the garlic. Add to peppers.

3. Pack the peppers into a wide mouth quart Mason jar. Pack about 1 cup at a time, layering with garlic and lime slices (if using them).

4. Pour in the brine, completely covering the peppers and leaving about an inch of space at the top of the jar.

5. Cover the peppers with a glass fermentation weight. Seal with a fermentation lid. Cover the jar with a natural cloth and store in a dark spot at room temperature.

6. Leave the jars to ferment for about 3 weeks. Check every few days to make sure things are brewing nicely. Open the lid and smell the peppers. They should smell tangy and sour. Keep the peppers submerged below the weight.

7. After three weeks, remove the fermentation lid and replace with a stainless steel lid. Store in a refrigerator.

Note: Peppers keep well for months. After that, they are still fine to eat, but may become softer. One way to use them at this point is to blend them as a hot sauce. Spice up salad dressings, dips, sandwich spreads, etc. Use the brine and all!

LIVE-FERMENTED HOT SAUCE

Live-Fermented Hot Sauce is a magic elixir! Peppers contain a wealth of antioxidants, dietary fiber, and vitamins. Capsaicin, found in jalapeño peppers, helps ward off certain types of cancer. Garlic is a natural defender, fighting off harmful bacteria, viruses, and other disease-causing microbes. Fermented hot sauce keeps well indefinitely. Its flavor mellows and deepens as it ages—even after a few years!

MAKES: 1 QUART

INGREDIENTS:

2 pounds hot peppers: jalapeños, habaneros, etc.

1 onion

1 bulb (several cloves) garlic

2 tablespoons finely ground sea salt

Good water: well, spring, or filtered, as needed

1. Remove the pepper stems and cut peppers into chunks. Peel the onion and garlic.

2. Place peppers, onion, garlic, and salt into a blender. Add enough water to reach the top of the veggies. Blend together, adding a bit more water as needed to create a pourable paste.

3. Pour the mixture in a wide mouth quart Mason jar, leaving about an inch of space from the top.

4. Seal with a fermentation lid. Cover the jar with a natural cloth and store in a dark spot at room temperature.

5. Leave the jars to ferment for about 6 to 8 weeks. Check every few days to make sure things are brewing nicely. Open the lid and smell the peppers. They should smell tangy and sour.

6. When the sauce tastes to your liking, remove the fermentation lid and replace with a stainless steel lid. Store in the refrigerator. Keeps well indefinitely.

Note: If the hot sauce is too hot, dilute it with sweetener and/or raw apple cider vinegar.

RAW PICKLED SUMMER SQUASH/ZUCCHINI

Pickled zucchini? Yes! Fermenting is a great way to utilize an overflowing garden harvest. This recipe uses plant leaves as fermentation weights, keeping the product immersed in brine. The leaves also host bacteria, which strengthen fermentation by inoculating the squash even further. Their microbiome also help keep the squash crispy and crunchy.

MAKES: 1 QUART

INGREDIENTS:

4–6 medium summer squash and/or zucchinis

2–3 teaspoons finely ground sea salt

1 pint good water: well, spring, or filtered

2 large leaves: grapevine, apple tree, or horseradish leaves, or outer cabbage layers*

Optional:

½ teaspoon red pepper flakes

Handful fresh dill

Several cloves peeled garlic

*Or use edible leaves from common yard and garden plants, such as plantain, dock, or dandelion (make sure they are properly identified and free of pesticides).

1. Gather a few large leaves (see recipe). Brush the leaves clean, but don't wash them.

2. Prepare the brine: Dissolve the salt into the water and set aside.

3. Slice the squash lengthwise and then into spears long enough to fit standing up in the jar. Lay the jar on its side and pack the spears snuggly, fitting shorter pieces in the middle.

4. Add the optional herbs, if using.

5. Push down the spears with the plant leaves.

6. Pour in the brine, submerging the plant leaves and leaving about an inch of space at the top of the jar.

7. Seal the mixture with a fermentation lid. Cover the jar with a natural cloth and store in a dark spot at room temperature.

8. Leave the jars to ferment for about 4 days. Check every day to make sure things ferment nicely. Open the lid. The spears should smell tangy and sour. Push the leaves down to keep the squash submerged.

9. When they taste to your liking, replace the fermentation lid with a stainless steel lid. Store in a refrigerator. Spears keep well for about 3 months.

Note: After 3 months, if the spears become mushy, puree them and then repurpose. Add to soups, sauces, salad dressings, dips, etc. Add the puree after cooking, ideally, to retain the health benefits. Pureed squash is a great secret source of fiber.

LIVE-FERMENTED SWEET POTATOES

Folks embracing paleo and keto diets are grateful for sweet potatoes. We use them raw and leave the skin on to save those precious microbes. The result will be a pretty crunchy pickle, like carrots, and quite digestible, due to the fermentation.

MAKES: 1 QUART

INGREDIENTS:

3–4 sweet potatoes, with any surface dirt rinsed off, sliced very thinly

1–2 tablespoons finely ground sea salt

1½-inch piece of fresh ginger, peeled and grated

1 large onion

Optional:

1 teaspoon cayenne powder OR 1 small fresh hot pepper, minced

Several whole cloves

¼ cup Ginger Bug (page 85)

1. Gently hand wash the sweet potatoes with water only, then slice thinly or shred.

2. Slice onions thinly. Peel and grate (or mince) fresh ginger. Finely chop fresh pepper.

3. Combine sweet potatoes with salt, onion, and spices. Mix well, tossing and kneading the mixture with your hands for several minutes. This encourages the release of juices, creating the natural brine. Taste the mixture and add more salt, if desired.

4. Once the brine begins to form, transfer the mixture to a wide mouth Mason jar. Add the mixture about a cup at a time, pressing firmly to release more juices. Use a kraut

pounder or wooden spoon. Repeat this process until all the mixture is in the jar and firmly pounded down, leaving about an inch of space near the top.

5. Cover the mixture with a glass fermentation weight. Press down firmly. Seal the mixture with a fermentation lid. Cover the jar with a natural cloth and store in a dark spot at room temperature.

6. Leave the jars to ferment for about two weeks. Check every day to make sure things are brewing nicely. Open the lid and smell the sweet potatoes. They should smell tangy, sweet, and sour. Push the weight down to keep the sweet potato mixture submerged below the weight.

7. When the mixture tastes to your liking, remove the fermentation weight and replace the fermentation lid with a stainless steel lid. Store in a refrigerator. Will keep well for about six months.

Note: If the sweet potatoes become mushy, puree them and then repurpose. Add to soups, sauces, salad dressings, dips, etc. Add the puree after cooking, ideally, to retain the health benefits. Pureed sweet potatoes are a great secret source of fiber.

RAW PICKLED BEETS

A beet taproot travels 50 feet into the ground, absorbing trace minerals rarely found in other veggies. This gives beets their trademark umami/soil flavor and beautiful color. Raw pickled beets provide tremendous health benefits and sustaining energy. They are great shredded too (see Live-Fermented Carrots on page 37 for method). In this recipe, we use crosscuts of beets instead of fermenting weights or leaves to submerge the veggies.

MAKES: 1 QUART

INGREDIENTS:

3–4 large beets

1 tablespoon finely ground sea salt

1 pint good water: well, spring, or filtered

Savory option: handful fresh dill, several garlic
    cloves, and a pinch of cayenne

Sweet option:

1 whole cinnamon stick and 3 whole cloves

1. Add the salt to the water and stir until the salt dissolves. Set aside.

2. Wash young beets or gently peel older beets. Slice beets into small sticks or cubes. Reserve the last few inches of the larger ends and slice into several crosscut pieces, like large coin circles.

3. In a wide mouth quart Mason jar, add the optional herbs first, and then pack the beets in tightly. Cover the top with a layer of crosscut beet slices.

4. Pour in the brine, leaving about an inch of space at the top of the jar. Seal with a fermentation lid. Cover the jar with a natural cloth and store in a dark spot at room temperature.

5. Leave the jars to ferment for about two weeks. Check every few days to make sure things are brewing nicely. Open the lid and smell the beets. They should smell tangy and fresh. Push the crosscut slices down to keep all the beets submerged.

6. After two weeks, remove the fermentation lid and replace with a stainless steel lid. Store in a refrigerator. Will keep well for over a year.

Note: Beets contain a high amount of sugar, which may begin converting to alcohol. Fermenting a quart at a time and then transferring to the refrigerator prevents this. Another way to reduce the alcohol formation is to combine the beets with a low-sugar vegetable such as turnips or cabbage.

RAW PICKLED DILLY BEANS

Dilly beans are commonly canned, but canning destroys valuable B-vitamins and enzymes. Raw pickled beans are crunchier, zestier, and always healthier! Use lots of fresh dill to make the flavor sing. Try snow or sugar snap peas for delicious alternatives.

MAKES: 1 QUART

INGREDIENTS:

1 pound young green beans

1 pint good water: well, spring, or filtered

2 teaspoons finely ground sea salt

1 tablespoon crushed red pepper flakes

Several garlic cloves, peeled and smashed

½ teaspoon whole black peppercorns

2 handfuls (about ½ cup) of fresh dill—flowering heads, preferably

1. Add the salt to the water and stir until the salt dissolves. Set aside.

2. Pinch the ends off the green beans.

3. Place the herbs into a wide mouth quart mason jar. Arrange the green beans into the jar on top of the herbs. Place them straight up (vertically) if they are long and thin, or sideways, if cut into sections.

4. Cover with brine solution, leaving about 1 inch of space at the top of jar. Seal with a fermentation lid. Cover the jar with a natural cloth and store in a dark spot at room temperature.

5. Leave the jar to ferment for about one month. Check every few days to make sure things are brewing nicely. Open the lid and smell the beans. They should smell tangy and sour.

6. After one month, remove the fermentation lid and replace with a stainless steel lid. Store in a refrigerator. These beans last well for over a year or more.

Note: Because the beans are packed tightly in the jar, a fermentation weight is not necessary. But feel free to use a weight to keep them submerged.

LIVE-FERMENTED
TOMATOES/TOMATO SAUCE

Fermented tomatoes are fantastic and versatile: use them to make pasta sauce, as a base for chili and soup, and blended as a zesty tomato juice. They also make a mean Bloody Mary. Because of their high acid content, tomatoes need less salt for fermenting (the acid helps keep the bacteria in check). This recipe uses cherry tomatoes, but any fresh whole or diced tomatoes will do.

MAKES: 1 QUART

INGREDIENTS:

2 pounds (about 2 pints) cherry tomatoes

2 teaspoons finely ground sea salt

1 pint good water: well, spring, or filtered

1 onion

Several cloves of garlic

Optional:

Fresh basil or other herbs

Sweet or hot peppers

1. Add the salt to the water and stir until the salt dissolves. Set aside.

2. Peel and slice the onion. Peel and chop the garlic.

3. Gently place the tomatoes into a wide mouth Mason jar, alternately layering with the garlic, onion, and optional ingredients. Fill the jar, leaving about an inch of space at the top.

4. Pour in the brine, covering the tomato mixture. Add a fermentation weight and seal with a fermentation lid. Cover the jar with a natural cloth and store in a dark spot at room temperature.

5. Leave the jars to ferment for at least one month. Check every few days to make sure things are brewing nicely. Open the lid and smell the tomatoes. They should smell tangy and sour. The high acid in the tomatoes should keep your microbiome environment nicely in check.

6. After one month, remove the fermentation weight and replace the lid with a stainless steel lid. Store in a refrigerator.

Note: Fermented tomatoes keep well indefinitely. Their flavor mellows and deepens as they age—even after a few years!

TOMATO SAUCE or JUICE:

Strain most of the brine into another jar. Save this "starter brine" for another ferment.

Puree the tomatoes, onion, and herbs. Add additional seasonings, based on the type of sauce or juice desired: Italian, Mexican, curry, hot peppers, etc.

If necessary, adjust the consistency by adding some of the saved brine.

LIVE-FERMENTED TURNIPS: *SAUERRUBEN*

Fermented turnips are delicious when shredded and fermented like sauerkraut (known as Sauerruben). My favorite turnip is the Gilfeather, an heirloom variety that is a sweet hybrid between the turnip and rutabaga. In the late 1800s, John Gilfeather (1865–1944) developed this delightful creation in Wardsboro, Vermont—home to the annual Gilfeather Turnip Festival and Contest.

MAKES: 1 QUART

INGREDIENTS:

3–4 medium turnips (about 4 cups total, after preparation)

2–3 teaspoons finely ground sea salt

Good water: well, spring, or filtered, if needed

1. Wash and gently peel the turnips. Shred the turnips into a big bowl.

2. Add 2 teaspoons sea salt and mix well with your hands. Feel free to punch, knead, and really handle this mixture for several minutes. This roughhousing begins releasing natural turnip juices, which begins the fermentation process. Taste the mixture and add more salt if desired.

3. Begin to add the turnip mixture to a wide mouth quart Mason jar. Transfer about a cup of turnips at a time, and then pound down using a kraut pounder or wooden spoon. Add another cup and pound down again. You will begin to see some juices rising to the top as you pound down. Repeat this process until all the mixture is in the jar and firmly pounded down, leaving about an inch of space near the top.

4. Cover the mixture with a glass fermentation weight, allowing the liquid to rise up to the weight. Seal the jar with a fermentation lid. Cover the jar with a natural cloth and store in a dark spot at room temperature.

5. Leave the jar to ferment for 3 to 4 weeks. Check every other day, making sure things are brewing nicely. Open the lid and smell the turnips. They should smell tangy and sour. Push the weight down to keep the turnips submerged below the weight.

6. When the turnips taste to your liking, remove the fermentation weight and replace the lid with a stainless steel lid. Store in a refrigerator. Turnips age well, sweetening and softening with time. They last well over a year. Enjoy using your new best condiment!

RAW PICKLED ROOT VEGETABLES

Pickled roots offer super flavor and texture, crunchier and zestier than the humble cucumber. Cut roots into sticks, circles, or wedges. Experiment with all kinds of root veggies—rutabagas, turnips, parsnips, or radishes. They're all delicious, healthy, and unique.

MAKES: 1 QUART

INGREDIENTS:

3–4 to medium turnips or any combination of root vegetables (about 4 cups total)

1 pint good water: well, spring, or filtered

2 teaspoons finely ground sea salt

Optional:

Several garlic cloves

Handful fresh herbs: dill, oregano, arugula, basil, etc.

1 hot pepper: jalapeño, habanero, etc.

1. Dissolve the salt into the water and stir until the salt dissolves. Set aside.

2. Cut roots into desired small shape (think 1 to 2 bites): sticks, wedges, circles, or dices.

3. If using optional herbs, place them first into a wide mouth quart Mason jar. Place the root pieces on top of the herbs and spices. Loosely pack the pieces into the jar. This allows the brine to immerse with the roots.

4. Pour the brine over the roots, pressing down lightly yet firmly. This releases air bubbles and submerges the pieces into the brine.

5. Add a fermentation weight and pour off any excess brine that might overflow. Leave about one inch of space from the top of the jar. Seal with a fermentation lid. Cover the jar with a natural cloth and store in a dark spot at room temperature.

6. Leave the jars at room temperature for 3 to 4 weeks. Check every few days to make sure things are brewing nicely. Open the lid and smell the turnips. They should smell tangy and sour. Push the weight down to keep the turnips submerged below the weight.

7. When roots taste to your liking, remove the fermentation weight and replace the fermenting lid with a stainless steel lid. Store in a refrigerator. Roots keep well for at least a year.

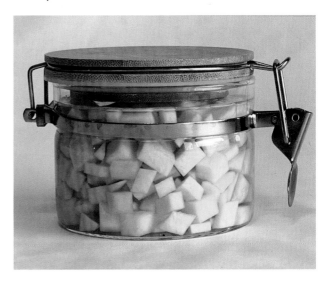

LIVE-FERMENTED SPICY VEGGIES: KIMCHI-*ISH*

Kimchi is a traditional Korean side dish made with Napa cabbage. Kimchi uses exotic ingredients such as mu *(Korean radish),* gochugaru *(Korean chili flakes), and* jeotgal *(salted seafood paste). Most kimchi recipes also use rice flour. This simpler grain-free version uses easily found ingredients: all the spicy goodness with local access!*

MAKES: 1 QUART

INGREDIENTS:

1 large head of Napa or Savoy cabbage

2 bunches of green onions

Several cloves of garlic

2 tablespoons fresh ginger root

2 fresh hot peppers

1–2 tablespoons finely ground sea salt

1. Prepare the veggies: Slice the cabbage and onions thinly. Mince the garlic, peppers, and ginger.

2. Combine all the veggies in a large bowl. Sprinkle salt onto the veggies and wait a few minutes. Gently massage the salt into the veggies for several minutes, releasing the cabbage's natural juices. Taste the mixture and add more salt, if desired.

3. Transfer the mixture into a wide mouth quart Mason jar. Add about a cup at a time, pressing the mixture firmly down to release more juices. Use a kraut pounder or wooden spoon to keep pressing the mixture down into the jar. Repeat this process until all the mixture is in the jar and firmly pounded down, leaving about an inch of space near the top.

4. Cover the mixture with a glass fermentation weight and press down firmly so the liquid rises around the weight. Seal the jar with a fermentation lid. Cover the jar with a natural cloth and store in a dark spot at room temperature.

5. Leave the jar to ferment for about one month. Check every few days, making sure things are brewing nicely. Open the lid and smell the veggies. They should smell strong and pungent—a bit overpowering perhaps, but fresh and invigorating (not putrid). Push the weight down to keep the mixture submerged below the liquid.

6. After about one month, remove the fermentation weight and replace the lid with a stainless steel lid. Store in a refrigerator. Kimchi will keep well indefinitely. Its flavor develops and mellows as it ages.

LIVE-FERMENTED GREENS: *GUNDRUK*

Gundruk, or fermented greens, are the sauerkraut of Nepal. Due to their high water content, greens become mushy when canned or frozen; but that high water content works well for the dry salt method in fermenting. Try other greens like Swiss chard, arugula, beet greens, and even zucchini leaves. Asian varieties like Mizuna, Tatsoi, etc. add a natural zest. Firmer greens like collards and broccoli leaves may need extra brine, plus more time to fully ferment. Be sure to save the stalks for the next recipe!

MAKES: 1 QUART

INGREDIENTS:

2–3 heads lettuce or other greens totaling 6 cups

1–2 tablespoons finely ground sea salt

Good water: well, spring, or filtered, as needed

Optional:

Garlic

Onions

Fresh herbs

Hot peppers

1. Gently rinse greens and remove any brown leaves. Cut or rip greens into large strips.

2. Put a layer of greens into a large bowl or ceramic crock. Sprinkle lightly with salt and repeat until all the greens and salt are added. Add optional ingredients, if using.

3. Let the greens and salt sit for a few minutes as moisture releases. Gently and thoroughly toss everything together for a few minutes. Taste and adjust, adding more salt if necessary.

4. Weigh down the greens in the same large container. Cover the mixture with large lettuce leaves or other green leaves. Cover everything with a heavy non-reactive plate, Pyrex pie dish, etc.—some flat dish that fits just inside the large container. If the dish rises up, add additional weight, such as another plate or a Mason jar filled with water. The natural brine from the greens begins to form immediately. After one day, the greens should be completely below the "brine line." If the greens are exposed, add some brine, with a ratio of 1 cup water to 1 teaspoon finely ground sea salt.

5. Cover container with a natural cloth and store in a dark spot at room temperature. Leave the jars to ferment for 3 or 4 days. Check every day, adjusting the weight to keep the lettuce submerged.

6. After 3 to 4 days, transfer the greens to a wide mouth quart Mason jar and seal with a stainless steel lid. Store in a refrigerator. Greens will last for several months.

Note: If the greens become mushy, puree them and then repurpose. Add to soups, sauces, salad dressings, dips, etc. Add the puree after cooking, ideally, to retain the health benefits. Pureed greens are a great source of vitamins, minerals, protein, and fiber.

Note: Greens make plenty of their own brine, so it's best to begin fermenting in a large vessel and then transfer into jars.

RAW PICKLED STALKS

After fermenting the greens, pickle their stalks! Usually discarded, stalks are untapped secret sources of vitamins, minerals, protein, and fibers. Utilize the whole of plants for optimal nutrition. Pickled stalks are a delightful alternative to cucumber pickles and root veggies. Most stalks work well: chard, kale, collards, broccoli, etc.

MAKES: 1 QUART

INGREDIENTS:

4 cups stalks

1 tablespoon finely ground sea salt

1 pint good water: well, spring, or filtered

Optional (one or all):

Handful of fresh herbs

Several garlic cloves

1 hot pepper

1. Add the salt to the water and stir until the salt dissolves. Set aside.

2. Slice the stalks away from the leafy greens of the chard (save the leafy greens for the previous recipe). Chop the stalks into short sticks, 1 to 3 inches in length.

3. Put the optional seasonings into the bottom of a quart-size Mason jar. Pack the stalks tightly into the jar.

4. Pour in the brine, completely covering the stalks and leaving about an inch of space at the top of the jar.

5. Seal with a fermentation lid. Cover the jar with a natural cloth and store in a dark spot at room temperature.

6. Leave the jars to ferment for about two weeks. Check every few days to make sure things are brewing nicely. Open the lid. The stalks should smell tangy and sour and taste crunchy but springy.

7. After two weeks, remove the fermentation lid and replace with a stainless steel lid. Store in a refrigerator.

Note: These Raw Pickled Stalks will keep well for months. After that, they are still fine to eat, but may become softer. One way to use them at this point is to blend them to use in salad dressings, dips, sandwich spreads, etc. Use the brine and all!

RAW PICKLED WEEDS

Some invasive weeds such as Japanese knotweed, garlic mustard, and lambsquarter, loathed by gardeners, are actually highly nutritious and delicious. Take advantage of their bounty by raw pickling, and you'll have an unlimited high-value food source. Garden schmarden—get foraging! Just be sure to have an expert with you the first time you pick in order to identify the plants safely.

MAKES: 1 QUART

INGREDIENTS:

Big bunch of Japanese knotweed—about 6 cups

1 tablespoon finely ground sea salt

1 pint good water: well, spring, or filtered

Optional:

1 bunch fresh herbs: dill, basil, parsley, arugula, etc.

Hot peppers

Garlic

1. Add the salt to the water and stir until the salt dissolves. Set aside.

2. Prepare the knotweed: gently rinse and slice stalks into small pieces about 3 inches long.

3. Place optional herbs and spices into the bottom of a wide mouth Mason jar.

4. Lay the jar on its side and pack in the herb pieces tightly, fitting in the shorter pieces in the middle.

5. Pour in the brine, leaving about an inch of space at the top of the jar.

6. Place a glass fermentation weight in the jar and press down, allowing the brine to cover the pieces. Seal with a fermentation lid.

Cover the jar with a natural cloth and store in a dark spot at room temperature.

7. Leave the jars to ferment for about 1 to 2 weeks. Check every few days to make sure things are brewing nicely. Open the lid and smell the knotweed pickles. They should smell tangy and sour. Check that the stalks are crispy; stop fermenting before they become soft.

8. When the weed pickles taste to your liking, remove the fermentation weight and lid and replace with a stainless steel lid. Store in a refrigerator. Will keep for months in the refrigerator.

Note: If the weeds become mushy, puree them and then repurpose. Add to soups, sauces, salad dressings, dips, etc. Add the puree after cooking, ideally, to retain the health benefits. Pureed weeds are a great source of vitamins, minerals, protein, and fiber.

RAW PICKLED WATERMELON RIND

Pickled watermelon rind is an old school treat, and raw pickling keeps them crunchy, tart, and zesty. Pickling rinds is a wonderful way to save that compost bucket from overflowing. Most recipes in this book yield one quart; but there's a lotta rind on watermelons, so utilize the whole shebang! Give out extra jars as unique gifts.

MAKES: 2-4 QUARTS

INGREDIENTS:

Rind from 1 watermelon

Brine ratio:

2 tablespoons finely ground sea salt

8 cups good water: well, spring, or filtered

Optional:

Fresh dill

Garlic cloves

Mustard, dill, or caraway seed

Whole allspice

1. Add the salt to the water and stir until the salt dissolves. Set aside.

2. Prepare the watermelon: Peel the dark green skin from the watermelon rinds. Cut the rinds into 1-inch squares or little sticks.

3. Measure the rinds. Each jar will contain about 3 cups of raw rinds. A medium-sized watermelon should make about 8 cups of rind, or 2 to 3 quarts.

4. If using, place the optional ingredients into the bottom of the wide mouth jars.

5. Place the rinds into the jars, on top of the optional herbs.

6. Pour in the brine, filling up to where the inch of space starts.

7. Place a glass fermentation weight in the jar and press down, allowing the brine to submerge the pieces. Add a fermentation weight and seal with a fermentation lid. Cover the jar with a natural cloth and store in a dark spot at room temperature.

8. Leave the jars to ferment for about three weeks. Check every few days to make sure things are brewing nicely. Open the lid and smell the rinds. They should smell fresh, tangy, and sour.

9. After three weeks, remove the fermentation weight and replace the lid with a stainless steel lid. Store in a refrigerator. Rinds will keep for months in the refrigerator.

BLUEBERRIES IN HONEY

Blueberries can also be dry salt fermented, but raw honey fermentation is a special method. The berries develop a slight effervescence, becoming tiny blue bubbles of tangy perfection. Live-fermented blueberries are delicious on pancakes, with yogurt and ice cream, added to smoothies, or spooned on toast. They also make a sweet-sour marinade for meats. Be sure to use raw honey, as it provides the good bacteria and vital enzymes needed for fermenting the berries.

MAKES: 1 QUART

INGREDIENTS:

2 cups blueberries

2 cups raw honey

Note: After several months, you can puree the berries and use as syrup.

1. Put the berries in a wide mouth Mason jar. Cover with the honey. Give the honey a few minutes to settle in.

2. Place a fermentation weight on top of the berries to keep them submerged under the honey. Seal with a fermentation lid. Cover the jar with a natural cloth and store in a dark spot at room temperature.

3. Leave the jars to ferment for about 5 to 7 days. Check the berries every day. Each day, they will begin to develop a slight effervescence.

4. Remove the fermentation weight and replace the lid with a stainless steel lid. Store in a refrigerator. Blueberries will keep for months in the refrigerator.

"FARM & FORAGE" FIRE CIDER

This recipe and the next are from Donica Krebs, a kindred spirit and fellow homesteader.

From Donica:

I came up with this fire cider recipe during the beginning of the pandemic. I wanted an immune protection option, but didn't want to go to the grocery store for traditional fire cider ingredients and risk exposure. So I dug through the pantry, garden, and woods to use what I had available. These ingredients are all pantry staples, common in a garden, or native and wild. Leaving out an ingredient or two if unavailable is perfectly acceptable.

MAKES: 1 QUART OR HOWEVER MUCH IS DESIRED

INGREDIENTS:

Equal parts of each:

Hot peppers, any variety

Ginger and/or turmeric

Oregano

Parsley

Pine needles

Horseradish root (or mustard greens as an alternative)

Garlic

Onion

Apple

Juniper berries

Raw honey

Good water: well, spring, or filtered

1. Chop all ingredients down until they can be easily packed into a quart jar.

2. Cover with water, cover the jar with a cloth, and ferment at room temperature. Stir daily.

3. Fire cider is done when it has ceased bubbling and the ingredients sink to the bottom. Strain, reserving the liquid.

4. Store in the refrigerator and take a shot glass full as needed.

Note: This recipe is in "parts" so you can make any quantity you wish, but for a small batch you could do 1 tablespoon of each ingredient. Use fresh herbs when available and dried when off-season.

FERMENTED HOT HONEY

This honey is medicinal but also delicious. It helps reduce cold and flu symptoms by clearing the sinuses, boosting immune function, and increasing circulation. Absolutely fantastic served on warm cornbread or biscuits.

MAKES: 1 CUP (8 OUNCES)

INGREDIENTS:

1 cup of local raw honey

¼ cup of chopped hot peppers (your choice)

1. Combine ingredients in a jar and stir.

2. Cover with a cloth and stir daily.

3. Ferment for 1 to 2 weeks or until bubbling has ceased. It will become runny, which is normal. Pepper chunks can be strained or left in. Store honey in the pantry.

CULTURED BEVERAGES

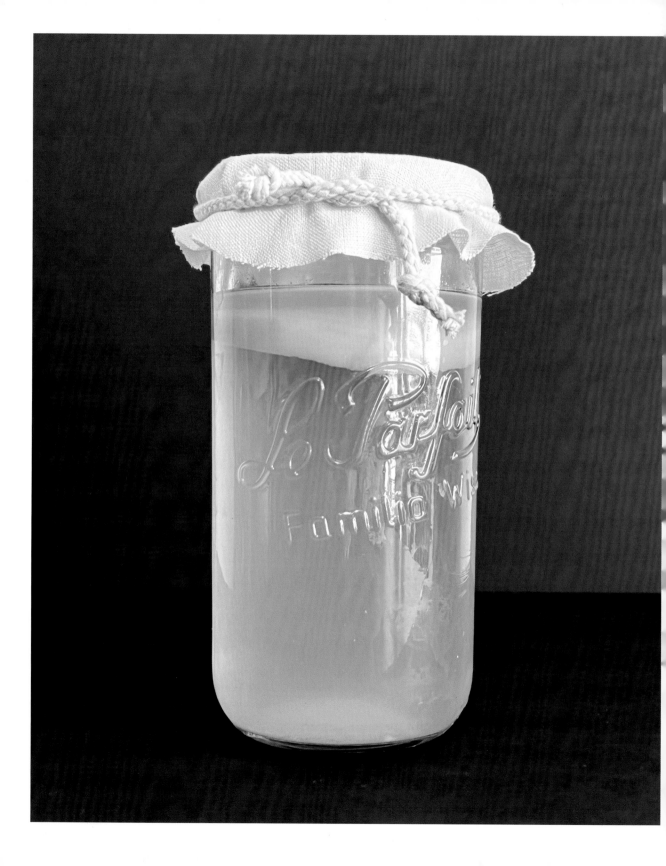

JUN TEA

Everyone knows kombucha; few know jun. Jun tea is a divine probiotic health tonic.

Jun (rhymes with "fun") is known affectionately as kombucha's cousin. It's also called "The Champagne of Kombucha" for its flavor and body: light, effervescent, gently sweet, and briskly sour. Jun's flavor is distinct—like an apple cider-lemonade-but-lighter experience. Less sour, less intense than kombucha. Tinier bubbles. Jun is a subtle, sublime experience.

Like kombucha, Jun tea is brewed with tea, sweetener, and something called a SCOBY, which is a starter in the fermenting process. SCOBY stands for: Symbiotic Culture of Bacteria and Yeast. SCOBYs are "rafts" made up of healthy microbes that work together—symbiotically—to create these magical elixirs. SCOBYs are also called "Mothers." Each time a batch is brewed, the mother reproduces another "baby"—a thin new SCOBY layer. Cool, huh?

The SCOBY's work is pretty straightforward: its yeasts consume sugars, which create alcohol, which is then consumed by SCOBY's bacteria. The bacteria also consume the tea's caffeine. When properly brewed, kombucha and jun are technically non-alcoholic and decaffeinated. (There may be trace amounts of alcohol left—less than 1%—the same amount commonly found in fruit juice.)

Although jun and kombucha brew the same way, they differ. Jun SCOBYs have different microbe colonies. Kombucha uses black tea and white sugar, while jun requires green tea and raw honey. Jun tea ferments best in cooler temperatures and takes less time to ferment than its cousin.

Jun tea is more nutritious due to its green tea and raw honey. Jun's SCOBY contains more bacteria, while kombucha's bacteria and yeast are more balanced. Jun contains Lactobacillus, the powerful probiotic bacteria. Kombucha contains Acetobactor, a bacteria with fewer probiotic properties.

Due to their differences, I tell my customers: If you like kombucha, you will love jun! And if you don't like kombucha, you will love jun!

Analysis of kombucha identified approximately 200 species of bacteria and over 100 species of yeast. This is much broader than any probiotic supplement on the market. Most probiotics contain less than 10 species. The Acetobacteraceae family makes up 99 percent of the bacteria and these are the ones that convert sugars and alcohol to acetic acid and gluconic acid. Starmarella was the dominant yeast, and it has been shown to not only consume sugars, but lipids as well, which can help with high cholesterol. This suggests that drinking kombucha with meals could help decrease some absorption of fats. (Kaashyap M, 2021)

MAKES: 1 GALLON

(Continued on next page . . .)

EQUIPMENT:

1 (1-gallon) "non-reactive" brewing vessel—glass, ceramic, or stainless steel are best

2 natural cloths for covering—cotton, linen, or hemp

1 (clean) rubber band

1 stainless "non-reactive" l pot—minimum size, 1 gallon

1 fine mesh strainer

INGREDIENTS:

1 Jun SCOBY (see "Sources" section)

5 teaspoons organic green tea

1 cup raw honey—local preferred

1 gallon good water: well, spring, or filtered

1 cup "starter tea" (included with the Jun SCOBY package)

IMPORTANT NOTE: The green tea *must* be cooled to room temperature before fermenting! This is key. If the tea is too hot, it kills the fragile microbiome. Room temperature keeps our tiny friends alive and well.

Step 1: Prepare the tea:

1. Bring the water to a boil in the stainless steel (non-reactive) pot. Add the green tea to the hot water. Let the tea steep for 7 to 10 minutes. *No longer.*

2. Strain the tea into the other non-reactive gallon container. **Cool the tea to room temperature** (it may sit overnight). **This is *important.***

3. When tea is room temperature, slowly add the raw honey, stirring steadily to fully dissolve the honey into the tea.

4. Place the SCOBY and starter liquid in with the sweetened tea. Gently stir the tea/ SCOBY mixture.

5. Cover the vessel with the two cloths and seal with a rubber band.

Step 2: Ferment:

6. Place the covered crock on a counter off by itself, ideally in a cool, dry, dark place. Let it sit undisturbed for 3 to 7 days. It's important to leave the Jun alone to brew in peace. (Jun likes to contemplate.)

7. After 3 days, carefully lift the cloths off and check the brew. Jun should smell tangy and fresh and slightly vinegary. If it still smells like sweet tea, leave it to brew for a couple more days, checking it every day. Note: the first brew may take a bit longer, like 7 to 14 days. Be patient and check every day. It will happen. The Jun is ready when its flavor is balanced, slightly sweet and sour. It no longer tastes like sweet tea, but it does not yet taste like vinegar.

8. When ready, gently pour most of the finished tea into glass jars. Leave about one cup in the vessel with the SCOBY.

9. Refrigerate the finished tea. Enjoy up to 8 ounces a day.

10. Jun Tea keeps well for months. It will cold-ferment a bit in the refrigerator. Like wine, its flavors improve with time, mellowing and marrying together.

Notes:

After the first batch, begin a "continuous brew," mixing another batch of sweet tea to the SCOBY and starter tea already in the brewing vessel. When that second batch is ready, it's drained into jars and stored in the refrigerator again, and the process continues.

If Jun is left out at room temperature, or if it ferments too long in the vessel, Jun will eventually turn to vinegar. If this happens, use it! Drink it diluted or cook with it as you would any vinegar. Use the vinegar to make Shrubs (page 91) and Jun-aigrette (page 147).

With every batch of Jun Tea, a new SCOBY baby grows. After a few months of brewing, all those babies pile up and the SCOBY culture will have grown to a few inches thick. Remove about half of the SCOBY raft and make Pureed SCOBY (page 79). Pureed SCOBY is a key ingredient in many fermenting recipes, such as the pet treats on page 151..

Green tea is generally considered a healthy source of polyphenols. Polyphenols are compounds found in plant foods that give them their color. They act as antioxidants as well as providing other health benefits. An analysis of kombucha found that total phenol content was 2.5× higher than in green tea. This suggests that fermentation produced additional polyphenols. (Kaashyap M, 2021)

PUREED SCOBY

Puree those saved SCOBY layers (see previous Jun Tea recipe) to create a secret cooking ingredient. Pureed SCOBY has a tart applesauce consistency and taste. In baking, SCOBY gives a spongy texture to pastries. In gluten-free cooking, Pureed SCOBY is a healthy substitute for xanthan gum. Eat it as-is—like applesauce—or add it to breads, soups, smoothies, salad dressings, and even beauty products.

MAKES: 1 PINT

INGREDIENTS:

1 cup jun SCOBYs or however many SCOBYs are used

Jun Tea (page 75) as needed

1. Cut SCOBYs into small pieces and place in a blender.

2. Add about ¼ cup Jun Tea for every 1 cup SCOBY pieces.

3. Blend well to form a puree resembling applesauce.

4. Transfer into mason jars. Store in the refrigerator. Pureed SCOBYs keep well for years. Give small jars as house-warming gifts for the liveliest conversations!

SECOND FERMENTS

A "second ferment" is the process of fermenting jun tea (or kombucha) a second time to add flavor and bubbly effervescence. Sweetener is necessary for second fermentation so that the remaining yeast can eat and make bubbles. Instead of refined white sugar, choose healthier, flavored options.

MAKES: 1 QUART

INGREDIENTS:

About 1 quart Jun Tea (page 75)

¼ cup sweetener: raw honey, maple syrup, or juice (see below)

Juice suggestions:

Apple cider

Pineapple

Orange

Elderberry

Other berry or fruits—fresh-squeezed or 100 percent juice preferable

Fermented tomato juice

Fresh vegetable juices

Ginger Bug (page 85)

1. Add sweetener to a quart-sized vessel, such as a Mason jar, maple syrup jug, #2 plastic bottle, or a wire lid "bale" bottle.

2. Fill the rest of the bottle with freshly brewed Jun Tea. Fill to about an inch from the top. Cap the bottle and cover with a natural cloth.

3. Leave in a warm place for up to 3 days. If the plastic bottle begins to bulge on the first day, *carefully* and gently twist the vessel open to release some of the fermented gases. Then reseal.

4. After 3 days, transfer bottles into the refrigerator. Serve cold. Sediment in the bottom of the vessel is the microbiome—healthy and potable. Still, some prefer to strain this.

Note: BE CAREFUL WHEN OPENING, as the off-gas may have built up pressure.

After opening, a second ferment's effervescence will last about one day. After that, continue to enjoy this (flat) flavored health tonic.

SAFETY NOTE: Generally, the off-gas produced in a second ferment is less than any commercial kinds of sodas, champagne, etc. But it's always good to use caution. Open the bottle slowly, with a towel covering the lid, for extra protection.

FRUIT SCRAP SODA

This is a wonderful recipe because it celebrates utilization. Rescuing discarded fruit scraps otherwise headed for the compost pile and turning them into delicious soda . . . cost-efficient and delightful! Collect fruit scraps (organic preferred) in a Ziploc bag. When you have about 4 cups of scraps, make some of this naturally healthy, simple beverage. Get scrappy!

MAKES: 2 LITERS

INGREDIENTS:

4 cups fruit scraps: *unwaxed* peels, skins, pits, soft
    fruit, etc.

1 cup Sucanat or other unrefined sugar*

1 teaspoon finely ground sea salt

Good water: well, spring, or filtered, as needed

*Coconut, date, or palm sugar, maple syrup, or
raw honey

1. Divide the fruit scraps, sugar, and salt into 2
    quart-size Mason jars, filling each jar about
    halfway.

2. Fill the jars with water, leaving about an
    inch of space at the top. Stir gently and well.

3. Cover with fermentation lids. Cover jars
    with a natural cloth and place in a dark
    space at room temperature.

4. Ferment for up to a week. Check the
    mixture daily for your desired taste: the
    longer it ferments, the fizzier and more sour
    it becomes.

5. Rack the mixture: strain it into new Mason
    jars or clean plastic soda/seltzer bottles.

6. Store in the refrigerator. Enjoy within 1 to
    2 weeks.

SAFTEY NOTE: Use caution when opening!
The soda's gas may cause pressure.

Note: To create more carbonation, add a bit
more sugar to the racked mixture, seal the
bottles tightly, and store in the refrigerator.

Note: Over time, the soda may flatten and sour.
Use this fresh raw vinegar to make shrub.
    What is a shrub? Check out the next recipe . . .

GINGER BUG

Ginger bug is a fermented base used to create ginger soda and ginger beer. It's zesty, fizzy, and oh so good. The "bug," also called the "ginger plant," is a type of SCOBY, but instead of starting with an established raft, ginger bugs are wild-fermented, created by pulling in the native microbes in one's natural environment or terroir. Ginger bug also makes a soothing tummy tonic, taken by the spoonful.

MAKES: 1 QUART

INGREDIENTS:

2 cups good water: well, spring, or filtered

4 tablespoons raw honey

About 2 inches of raw fresh organic ginger root

Additional water, honey, and ginger root for maintenance

1. Slice the ginger root (leave the skin on).

2. Blend the water, honey, and ginger slices.

3. Pour the mixture into a quart Mason jar.

4. Seal with a stainless steel lid. Place on the counter, gently stirring/shaking a few times per day.

5. Feed your bug every few days: blend together 1 tablespoon of raw honey, 1 inch sliced ginger, and ¼ cup water, and then add to the ginger bug and stir well. The bug will grow vigorously, bubbling in about a week. A thin SCOBY layer may form. After the first week, the bug is ready to drink. As it ages, however, its flavor begins to develop a "mature" quality—a spicier, yet mellower flavor.

6. Store in the refrigerator for about a month to continue a cold-fermenting process.

7. To serve, strain off some of the bug in a glass, mix with water, seltzer, or juice, and enjoy.

Note: For a continuous brew, enjoy the bug until there is about ¼ cup left at the bottom of the jar. Then remove from the refrigerator and begin the process again.

FIZZY LEMONADE

Fizzy lemonade is lovely—tangy and satisfying. Lemons cleanse the liver and kidneys, help detoxify organs, and improve digestion. This recipe uses sugar syrup—sugar dissolved into water—and so requires some warming of the water. Before beginning the fermentation, cooling the liquid mixture to room temperature is key. If water is too hot, it kills the fragile microbiome. Room temperatures keep our tiny friends alive and well.

MAKES: 1 QUART

INGREDIENTS:

4 cups water

¼ cup Sucanat or other unrefined sugar*

Juice from 2–3 organic whole lemons

¼ cup sweet fermented beverage: Jun Tea (page 75), Raw Apple Cider Vinegar (page 89), Fruit Scrap Soda (page 83), or Ginger Bug (page 85)

*Coconut, date, or palm sugar, maple syrup, or raw honey

1. Warm 1 cup of water and place in a glass or non-reactive bowl.

2. Add the sugar into the warm water, stirring well until completely dissolved. This creates the sugar syrup.

3. Add the remaining 3 cups of cool water. Check the mixture to make sure it is room temperature. It should feel cool to the touch. If it's too warm, *wait*.

4. Juice the lemons, keeping their outer shells. Add the lemon juice, lemon shells, and fermented beverage to the sugar-syrup. Stir well.

5. Cover loosely with a natural cloth and let sit overnight at room temperature.

6. Transfer the mixture into bottle(s): Wire bale bottles or #2 recyclable plastic soda bottles work well.

7. Seal the bottle(s). Cover the bottle(s) with a natural cloth and place on the counter for 2 to 3 days.

8. If the bottle(s) are noticeably expanding, gently loosen their lids to release a bit of gas, and then retighten the lids.

9. After 2 to 3 days, transfer bottle(s) to the refrigerator.

Note: As microbes eat the sugar, they release carbon dioxide, which carbonates the beverage. If too much sugar is added or fermentation goes too long, the bottles may produce a lot of fizzing when opening. In rare cases, they may even explode. It's a good idea to ferment natural sodas in a cardboard box, garage, or basement. BE CAREFUL!

RAW APPLE CIDER VINEGAR (ACV)

This apple cider vinegar recipe is contributed from Donica Krebs. Donica gave me my first kombucha SCOBY when I moved to Tennessee, and we've been fermenting buddies ever since. Raw apple cider vinegar (ACV) is used frequently as a starter in beverage recipes and is a staple in every healthy kitchen.

MAKES: 1 QUART (OR AS MUCH AS DESIRED)

INGREDIENTS:

Organic *unwaxed* apples (any amount
   you have on hand)

Filtered water

Note: All grocery store apples, including organic ones, are wax-coated. Usually petroleum based, sometimes soy-based waxes are applied to keep apples fresh. The wax will float to the top and ruin your ACV. Find unwaxed apples from a local farm. If that's not an available option, find organic store apples and peel them, discarding the peels.

1. Rinse and roughly chop whole apples—core, seeds, stems, and all. Remove buggy or mushy spots, but everything else can stay.

2. Pack apples into a jar of appropriate size to fit them in.

3. Cover the apples, barely, with filtered water. Cover the jar with a cloth.

4. Stir at least once a day, more often if you have the time.

5. Ferment at room temperature until the bubbling ceases and the apples sink to the bottom.

6. Strain and reserve liquid.

7. Store in glass bottles in a cool dark place. Keeps indefinitely.

Animal studies have shown that daily consumption of apple cider vinegar reduced lipid levels and blood sugar levels in rats that were fed a high calorie diet. (Ousaaid et al, 2020)

SHRUB OR SWITCHEL

A shrub, also called switchel, is sweet vinegar syrup, used as a base for other beverages. The sweet-sour flavor combination is invigorating. In Vermont, we make switchels with maple syrup. Use shrubs like ginger bugs—adding directly to water, seltzer, or naturally fermented soda—for a refreshing treat.

MAKES: 1 PINT

INGREDIENTS:

1 cup any fruit

1 cup raw honey, maple syrup, or other sugar*

1 cup Raw Apple Cider Vinegar (page 89)

*Unrefined sugars are best, like coconut, date, or palm sugar, or Sucanat (cane sugar)

1. Gently rinse the fruit. Place fruit in a bowl and smash it with clean hands or a wooden spoon. (If using hands, wash them before the next step!)

2. Sprinkle in the sugar, stirring well to combine everything into fruit slurry.

3. Cover the slurry with plastic wrap or beeswax wrap. Cover again with a natural cloth. Let slurry sit out on a counter at room temperature overnight.

4. Transfer to the refrigerator and let sit about 2 days, cold-fermenting. The slurry will begin to separate, developing a syrup.

5. Strain the syrup, pressing lightly on the solids to release all the juice.

6. Add the vinegar and stir well. Make sure the sugar is fully dissolved.

7. Transfer into a clean bottle. Cap, shake well, and refrigerate.

8. Check the shrub periodically. Some sugar may settle out onto the bottom of the bottle. If so, shake well to combine. Eventually, the acids in the juice and vinegar will dissolve the sugar.

9. To serve, add 1 to 3 tablespoons of shrub to water, seltzer, or juice and enjoy. Shrub also makes a tangy marinade for meats and plant-based proteins like tofu.

Note: Try making oxymels–healthy herbal elixirs! Oxymels are shrubs made with raw honey, vinegar, and your favorite herb(s) instead of fruit.

BEET KVASS

Kvass, a fermented vegetable drink, is the traditional beverage in many cultures. Kvass is another utilization staple: while the recipe calls for whole beets, other vegetable peels and scraps also work well. Kvass, like fruit soda, is an easy and inexpensive way to drink cultured beverages. Collect veggie scraps in a Ziploc bag. When you have about 4 cups of scraps, make some of this naturally healthy, simple beverage. Get scrappy!

MAKES: 1 QUART

INGREDIENTS:

2–3 medium beets

2–3 teaspoons finely ground sea salt

1 pint good water: well, spring, or filtered

1. Rinse the beets, leaving the skins on. Dice beets into large (½-inch) pieces. Place in a wide mouth quart Mason jar.

2. Add the salt. Fill the jar with water, leaving about 1 inch of space near the top.

3. Stir the mixture and taste. Add more salt if desired.

4. Seal with a fermentation lid. Cover the jar with natural cloth and store in a dark spot at room temperature.

5. Leave the jar to ferment for 1 to 2 weeks. Check every few days to make sure things are brewing nicely. Open the lid and smell the beets. They should smell tangy and sour. For a zestier flavor, ferment the entire 2 weeks (or more).

6. When ready, remove the fermentation lid and replace with a stainless steel lid. Store in the refrigerator. Kvass keeps well for a few weeks.

7. To drink, carefully pour out the liquid, keeping the beets in the jar. The kvass flavor will continue to develop as it ages.

Note: When the kvass has been consumed, make a second, weaker batch: refill the jar with water and salt and re-ferment for two days at room temperature.

A study on kvass found that it reduced symptoms of functional dyspepsia. Laboratory testing found that it modified gastrointestinal hormone levels which improved the functioning of the digestive tract. (Shao et al, 2022)

COLD-FERMENTED COOLER TEA/TISANE

For years, I've made "sun tea" by shoving fresh herbs into a jar, adding water, and setting the jar outside in the sun to brew. The tea has always been fine. But respectfully, some feel that leaving food and water out without salt or starters may allow bad bacteria to grow. Therefore, a safe alternative is Cooler Tea, which uses cold fermentation.

Cold-fermented tea uses a continuous-brew process: brew overnight in the refrigerator and pour off a glass the next day. Refill the jar with water and enjoy a glass every day for a few weeks. To develop a stronger flavor, cold-ferment the tea for a few days before drinking.

MAKES: 1 QUART OR WHATEVER AMOUNT IS DESIRED

INGREDIENTS:

Fresh or dried herbs or spices

1 quart good water: well, spring, or filtered

1. Fill a Mason jar or other non-reactive container with a variety of herbs. Add water almost to the top.

2. Seal the jar with a stainless steel lid. Place the container in the refrigerator overnight.

3. The next day, strain a cup of tea and refill the jar with water.

4. Continue enjoying this batch for a few weeks. After 2 to 3 weeks, strain off the tea, compost the herbs, and begin a new batch.

SWEET POTATO FLY

Fermented sweet potato soda? Yikes or yes! Spicy lacto-fermented Sweet Potato Fly is a surprising treat, reminiscent of ginger ale. It's the original "pumpkin spice" treat. Fly is a wonderful, nutrient-packed drink for autumn days and holiday nights.

MAKES: ½ GALLON OR 8 (8-OUNCE) SERVINGS

INGREDIENTS:

2 large organic sweet potatoes (about 4 cups)

½ gallon good water: well, spring, or filtered

2 cups Sucanat or other unrefined sugar*

½ cup Raw Apple Cider Vinegar (page 89) or Jun Tea (page 75)**

2 tablespoons ginger bug (page 85) OR
   1 tablespoon fresh organic ginger root

2 whole cinnamon sticks

1 teaspoon ground nutmeg or 1 whole nutmeg

1 eggshell, cleaned and crushed ("pasture-raised" or local farm egg)

*Coconut, date, or palm sugar, maple syrup, or raw honey

**Or 2 organic lemons, zested and juiced

1. Coarsely grate sweet potatoes. Rinse them in a colander under cold water to remove much of the starch.

2. In a large non-reactive container (glass, ceramic, or stainless steel), combine grated sweet potatoes and the rest of the ingredients. Stir well and cover with a beeswax wrap or cheesecloth secured with a clean rubber band. Loosely cover the entire container with a natural cloth.

3. Leave the covered jar in a dark warm place for 3 to 5 days, gently swishing the potato slurry once a day. The liquid becomes slightly fizzy and tangy.

4. Strain the liquid into a bottle or Mason jar. Seal well. Store in the refrigerator. Serve cold.

5. Fly keeps well for a few weeks. If it begins to taste funky, use the liquid as a soup base for curried soup or chili, or use as an alternative to tomato sauce.

LIVE-FERMENTED HORCHATA

Agua de Horchata, or Horchata, is a refreshing Mexican rice and cinnamon drink, lightly creamy and spicy. Traditional recipes simply cook the rice, but this live-fermented version adds healthy tanginess from the probiotics, creating something like a fizzy milkshake. Fermented Horchata is great in smoothies. Kids love it!

MAKES: ½ GALLON OR 8 (8-OUNCE) SERVINGS

INGREDIENTS:

1 cup organic rice grains

1 cinnamon stick, broken in a few pieces

½ cup raw honey or maple syrup

1 teaspoon pure vanilla

8 cups good water: well, spring, or filtered

1. Combine the rice, cinnamon stick, and 4 cups of water in a medium saucepan.

2. Place over medium heat, bring to a boil, and reduce to a simmer. Simmer for 15 minutes, and then remove from heat.

3. Cover with a natural cloth and let sit out at room temperature overnight.

4. The next day, remove the cinnamon stick pieces and set aside.

5. Stir in the remaining 4 cups of water. Blend the rice mixture, and then strain. The mixture will be pulpy.

6. Add the cinnamon stick pieces back to the mixture, and then add the sweetener and vanilla. Stir gently until fully combined.

7. Pour the mixture into two wide mouth quart mason jars (or one wide mouth half-gallon jar). If using two jars, divide the cinnamon stick pieces.

8. Seal the jar(s) with a fermenting lid. Cover the jar(s) with a natural cloth. Place on the counter in a dark spot at room temperature.

9. Ferment for 4 to 7 days, checking daily until the mixture tastes tangy and tiny bubbles begin to form.

10. Remove the fermenting lid(s) and replace with a stainless steel lid(s).

11. Store in the refrigerator. Fermented Horchata keeps well for a few weeks.

12. To serve: shake well and serve over ice.

Notes: The mixture may continue to cold-ferment, and the taste may become overly sour. If so, add a bit of sweetener and/or dilute with dairy or nut milk to mellow out the flavor.

Horchata can also be fermented in seltzer bottles or wire bale lid containers.

NUT MILK

Nut milk is a creamy non-dairy beverage that is extremely versatile. Use it in cereal, smoothies, and baking. It also makes excellent plant-based cheeses. Fermented nut milk is zippy and satisfying, plus costs less to make than those pre-packaged milks.

MAKES: 1 QUART

INGREDIENTS:

1 cup raw, unsalted sunflower seeds or any nut or seed

3 cups good water (for soaking sunflower seeds): well, spring, or filtered

4 cups good water (for making milk): well, spring, or filtered

Optional:

Sugar to taste

Pure vanilla to taste

1. Soak the sunflower seeds overnight in the soaking water.

2. Drain and discard the soaking water.

3. Blend the seeds with 4 cups water until smooth.

4. Pour into jars or bottles.

5. Refrigerate. Milk keeps well for about one week.

6. Optional, for thinner, creamier milk: strain the seed mixture using cheesecloth or a nut milk bag. A tight-weave cloth is preferable, as squeezing it allows more milk to drain through.

Note: After one week, a stronger sour flavor may develop that may be unpleasing to drink. If so, it's fine to use the fermented milk in smoothies or baked goods.

TRADITIONAL BREAD KVASS

Bread kvass is an archaic health tonic from Eastern Europe that utilizes old bread. It has an intoxicating flavor—slightly boozy and weirdly delicious, like kefir, with a mild cola flavor and fizz. It's easy to make and full of probiotic goodness. All that's needed is bread, sweetener, and water. The microbes do the rest! Kvass can be flavored with fruit, herbs, spices, and roots. One traditional flavoring is with fresh mint and lemon.

MAKES: ½ GALLON

INGREDIENTS:

2 cups stale bread*

1 cup raw honey

8 cups good water: well, spring, or filtered

*Try the Jun Sourdough Bread (page 131), rye bread, or other sourdough bread

1. Boil the water and set aside to cool. Water should be warm to the touch, not hot!

2. Cut the bread into chunks.

3. Combine honey with 2 cups of warm water, mixing until the honey dissolves completely.

4. Place bread chunks into a wide mouth half-gallon jar (or 2 wide mouth quart Mason jars), and pour the honey-water over the bread.

5. Fill the jar with the remaining warm water, up to an inch from the top of the jar. Stir well.

6. Seal with a fermentation lid. Cover the jar with natural cloth and store in a dark spot at room temperature. Leave the jar(s) to ferment for about 1 week.

7. Check every day to release pressure. The bread will begin to smell tangy and sour. Taste the brew every few days until it reaches a desired flavor—tart, subtle, and pleasing.

8. After 1 week—or when desired flavor is reached—strain the Kvass into Mason jars or clean reusable plastic bottles.

9. Store in a refrigerator. Serve chilled.

10. Kvass keeps well for a few weeks.

Note: For a "second ferment"—more carbonation and a headier flavor—add several raisins into the kvass after straining. Close the bottle airtight and ferment at room temperature for 1 or 2 more days, then store in the refrigerator.

REJUVELAC

Ann Wigmore, sprout queen of the 70s, introduced many a hippy to this simple yet exotic elixir. Rejuvelac is made from sprouted wheat berries and is a delicious, fresh-tasting drink. Many people with gluten issues find they can tolerate fermented organic wheat products—or any fermented grain, for that matter. The fermentation extracts most of the nutrients from the berries, so compost the used berries and feed the garden.

MAKES: 2 QUARTS

INGREDIENTS:

½ cup organic wheat berries (whole grain kernels)

4 cups good water: well, spring, or filtered

Step 1: Sprout the berries:

1. Place the wheat kernels into a wide mouth quart mason jar.

2. Add water, filling a few inches above the kernels.

3. Cover with a sprouting lid or cheesecloth secured with a rubber band. Leave out overnight.

4. The next day, drain the water and tip the covered jar over. One good way is to lean the jar in a shallow bowl, so that it lays upright at a slanted angle. This allows the remaining water to slowly drain out.

5. Rinse the kernels 2 to 3 times a day, draining the water and then inverting the jar again to further drain the remaining water.

6. Continue this process for 2 to 3 days, until the wheat berries begin to sprout and their little "sprout tails" appear. At this point, the berries are ready for fermenting.

Step 2: Ferment the berries:

7. Keeping the sprouted wheat berries in the Mason jar, fill the jar with water.

8. Cover with a fermentation lid or cheesecloth secured with a rubber band. Cover with a natural cloth.

9. Leave the covered jar in a warm place for 2 days. Gently stir once a day. The liquid becomes slightly fizzy and turns cloudy. It will taste tangy yet crisp, and maybe a bit citrusy: "good funky."

10. Strain the liquid into a clean bottle or Mason jar. Store in the refrigerator.

11. Rejuvelac keeps well for about a week.

Note: The berries may be reused for another batch. For the second round, ferment for only 24 hours.

RECIPES USING FERMENTED FOODS

These recipes have been designed to use the live-fermented ingredients in the previous sections. Always feel free to substitute any of the fermented ingredients for raw or regular counterparts. For instance, if a recipe calls for live-fermented applesauce, it's fine to use regular applesauce.

In fact, all of the recipes included here are templates or starting-off points, where the cook is free to add optional ingredients, use substitutes, and interchange raw food products for fermented ones. However, if you have created some of the previous live-fermented foods and beverages, have fun and experiment with them! Add them to these recipes to experience deeper, unique flavors that are unattainable with simple raw and cooked ingredients.

Enjoy!

ALIVE APPLESAUCE

Live-fermented applesauce is a nutritional wonder. Apples have prebiotics—fiber-rich substances that feed the probiotic bacteria in our guts. Alive applesauce is synbiotic—both pre- and probiotic, a double whammy. Powerful but simple, Alive Applesauce is delicious on its own. It's great in baking and smoothies and also makes a highly digestible baby food.

MAKES: 1 QUART

INGREDIENTS:

4–6 raw apples OR 3 cups fermented apples

1–2 tablespoons sweet fermented beverage "starter:" Jun Tea (page 75), Ginger Bug (page 85), Fizzy Lemonade (page 87), or Fruit Scrap Soda (page 83)

¼ cup Pureed SCOBY (page 79)

Optional spices:

Cinnamon

Ginger

Cloves

Nutmeg

Note: As live applesauce cold-ferments in the refrigerator, its flavor sours and puckers. To avoid this flavor, enjoy within a few days. If it becomes too sour, use in smoothies or baking recipes.

1. If using raw apples: chop into small pieces.

2. Place all ingredients in a blender or food processor. Pulse until pureed smooth. If too thick, add another tablespoon of Jun Tea or Ginger Bug.

3. Place in a quart Mason jar. Seal with a stainless steel lid, cover with a natural cloth, and leave out overnight at room temperature.

4. The next day, transfer to the refrigerator.

5. Store in the refrigerator for up to 1 week.

BANANA SMASH

The fermented banana is a zippy delight: smooth yet fizzy, sweet and zesty. Fermented bananas may benefit the body in so many ways: they're good for the heart, elevate mood, stimulate digestion, aid in weight loss, boost metabolism, regulate blood sugar levels, improve vision, help bones absorb calcium, and even help prevent some cancers. All that, plus they are yummy! Eat with yogurt, in a smoothie, as healthy baby food, or use in baking.

MAKES: 1 QUART

INGREDIENTS:

4–5 ripe organic bananas

1 teaspoon finely ground sea salt

1 cup good water: well, spring, or filtered

2 tablespoons fermented beverage "starter:" Raw Apple Cider Vinegar (page 89), Jun Tea (page 75), Fizzy Lemonade (page 87), or Pureed SCOBY (page 79)

1 tablespoon Sucanat or other unrefined sugar*

1 teaspoon cinnamon

*Coconut, date, or palm sugar, maple syrup, or raw honey

1. Add the salt into the water and stir until the salt dissolves. Set aside.

2. Prepare the bananas: Peel and then cut into thick slices into a bowl.

3. Add the starter, sugar, and cinnamon. Gently combine ingredients together with a wooden spoon or clean hands.

4. Transfer the banana mixture into a wide mouth quart Mason jar. Cover with the brine, leaving about 1 inch of space from the top.

5. Seal with a fermentation lid. Cover the jar with natural cloth and store in a dark spot at room temperature. Leave the jars to ferment for about 4 to 5 days. Check daily. The bananas develop tiny bubbles and a slight effervescence. They will smell sweet and tangy. Tasting them, they will become fizzy and tart.

6. After 4 to 5 days, remove the fermentation lid and replace with a stainless steel lid. Some of the brine can be stored with the bananas or strained and reused for another batch. Store in a refrigerator. Bananas keep nicely for a few months in the refrigerator. They will keep longer if frozen.

FRUIT COMPOTE OR "PIE-IN-A-JAR"

"An apple a day keeps the doctor away." Live-fermented fruits live up to that adage, being synbiotic—rich in both probiotics and prebiotics. This recipe makes a hybrid compote/jam, versatile and adaptable, smooth or chunky. Compote is delicious served plain, with yogurt, on toast, or blended in smoothies. This recipe uses apples, but try any combination of fruit. As an added bonus, compote makes a ready-made pie filling or fruit crisp; so keep a few jars on-hand all year long.

MAKES: 1 QUART

INGREDIENTS:

4–5 apples or other fruit (4 cups, total)

½ cup maple syrup or raw honey

½ teaspoon finely ground sea salt

2 tablespoons fermented beverage "starter:" Jun Tea (page 75), Beet Kvass (page 93), Sweet Potato Fly (page 97), etc.

Good water, as needed: well, spring, or filtered

Optional (use any or all):

1 cinnamon stick

3–4 whole cloves

A few slices of fresh raw ginger root

1 tablespoon Pureed SCOBY (page 79)

1. Core apples and slice them thinly. Skin can be left on or peeled.

2. Place the sliced apples in a big bowl and add the sweetener, salt, and fermented beverage. Gently toss together until a sweet liquid develops.

3. Place the apple mixture into a wide mouth quart Mason jar. Place the fermentation weight on top of the apples to submerge them under the sweet liquid. If needed, add some water.

4. Seal with a fermentation lid. Cover the jar with a natural cloth and store in a dark spot at room temperature.

5. Ferment for about 3 to 5 days. Check the fruit every day. It will develop tiny bubbles and a slight effervescence, smell tangy, and taste sweetly tart.

6. When ready, remove the fermentation weight and lid. Replace with a stainless steel lid. Store in a refrigerator. Will keep for a few months in the refrigerator.

Note: The fruit is still fine to eat after a few months, but may become mushy. Use it in smoothies and baking, but first remove the cinnamon stick and/or whole cloves!

LIVE-FERMENTED JAM

Ditch the canning! Lacto-fermented jams increase vitamins, enzymes, and probiotics, making these preserves even better than the raw fruit. Berries work well, but experiment with any kind of fruit. Add unrefined sugar to further improve the health benefits.

MAKES: 1 QUART/ 4 (8-OUNCE) JARS

INGREDIENTS:

4 cups fresh raspberries

¼ cup Sucanat or other unrefined sugar*

1 teaspoon finely ground sea salt

¼ cup Alive Applesauce (page 108)**

4 tablespoons fruity fermented beverage "starter:" Fruit Scrap Soda (page 83), Fizzy Lemonade (page 87), or Jun Tea (page 75)

*Coconut, date, or palm sugar, maple syrup, or raw honey

**Substitutions: Fruit Compote (page 111) or Pureed SCOBY (page 79).

May also use ¼ cup raw shredded apple.

1. Gently pour berries in a bowl. Remove any stems and bruised or moldy berries.

2. Mash all ingredients together until berries are crushed yet chunky.

3. Place in a wide mouth quart Mason jar, leaving an inch of space near the top of the jar.

4. Seal with a fermentation lid. Cover the jar with a natural cloth and store in a dark spot at room temperature.

5. Leave the jars to ferment for about 2 to 3 days. The berries will develop tiny bubbles and a slight effervescence. They will smell slightly sour and taste lightly fizzy.

6. Remove the fermentation lid and replace with a stainless steel lid. Jam can also be transferred into smaller jars. Store in a refrigerator. Jam keeps well for a few months. Jam also freezes well for longer term storage.

LIVE-FERMENTED SMOOTHIES

Hippy Hippy Shakes! Smoothies are creamy shakes, great for breakfast or a light meal. They are incredibly flexible—just about any fruit and any liquid can be used. Veggies, nuts, and seeds also enrich flavor and texture. Live-fermented ingredients give smoothies a signature tang and health punch. For thicker smoothies, add some frozen fruit. This recipe makes two smoothies, because it's always nice to make an extra one for a friend.

MAKES: 2 SMALL SMOOTHIES OR 1 LARGE SMOOTHIE

INGREDIENTS:

1 cup fermented, fresh, or frozen fruit

1 cup fermented Nut Milk (page 101) or fermented
   liquid of choice (except Fire Cider!)

1–2 teaspoons maple syrup or raw honey to taste

Optional:

¼ cup yogurt, kefir, or sour cream

1 tablespoon Pureed SCOBY (page 79)

1 tablespoon Live-Fermented Jam (page 113) or
   Fruit Compote (page 111)

1 tablespoon nuts, seeds, or nut butter

¼ cup "sweet" raw or fermented veggies: Live-
   Fermented Carrots (page 37), Live-Fermented
   Sweet Potatoes (page 47), or Raw Pickled Beets
   (page 49)

1. Blend all ingredients in a high-speed
   blender. Begin on low speed, progress to
   medium and high, then back down to low.
   Blend for at least 60 seconds.

2. Pour into a glass and enjoy!

3. Store extra smoothie in a sealed glass jar.
   Smoothies keep well in the refrigerator for a
   few days.

RAW PICKLED SALSA

Raw pickled salsa retains all the wonderful health benefits of raw veggies with the added benefits of lacto-fermentation. Use the freshest organic ingredients you can find, especially the tomatoes. It makes all the difference in flavor. Pureed salsa spices up salad dressings, dips, sandwich spreads, etc.

MAKES: 1 QUART OR 2 PINT JARS

INGREDIENTS:

4 large tomatoes (or Live-Fermented Tomatoes, page 53)

1 large onion (or ½ cup Fermented Onions, page 35)

1 green pepper

2 jalapeños (or ¼ cup Raw Pickled Peppers, page 41)

1 tablespoon Raw Pickled Garlic (page 39) or 3 cloves raw garlic

1 bunch fresh cilantro

1 tablespoon Raw Apple Cider Vinegar (page 89) or Jun Tea (page 75)

Juice of 1 fresh lime

1 tablespoon Live-Fermented Hot Sauce (page 43)

Finely ground sea salt and freshly ground black pepper to taste

Optional:

2 tablespoons Pureed SCOBY (page 79)

½ cup fresh or frozen corn kernels

1. If using fresh veggies: dice tomatoes, onion, and peppers. Finely chop garlic and cilantro. Place all into a bowl.

2. Add vinegar, lime juice, hot sauce, salt and pepper (and optional ingredients). Mix well, stirring gently, until combined.

3. Place mixture into 2 wide mouth pint Mason jars or 1 quart-size jar.

4. Seal with fermentation lids. Cover the jars with a natural cloth and store in a dark spot at room temperature.

5. Let salsa ferment for 1 to 2 weeks. Check the mixture every few days. Open the lid. The salsa should smell tangy and fresh. The high acid in the tomatoes should keep your microbiome environment nicely in check.

6. Ferment until it tastes to your liking. Remove the fermentation lids and replace with stainless steel lids. Store the jars in a refrigerator. Fermented salsa keeps well indefinitely. Its flavor mellows and deepens as it ages—even after a few years!

Note: Make gazpacho by adding a touch of sweetener and serving as-is or blended.
   (A traditional Gazpacho recipe can be found on page 123.)

HEALTHIER HUMMUS

Hummus is a delicious lemony, garlic-y bean dip, used for dips and spreads and in other creative ways. Make salad dressings, thicken soup, and toss in pasta for a quick sauce. If the garlic is omitted, hummus is a great nut butter substitute in baking. Fermented hummus is elevated: creamier, tangier, and healthier than its traditional version. Fermenting beans breaks down carbohydrates to improve their digestion (less gas).

MAKES: 1 QUART

INGREDIENTS:

3 cups garbanzo beans, raw or canned

⅓ cup lemon juice

⅓ cup tahini (sesame paste)

2 tablespoons Raw Pickled Garlic (page 39)

1 teaspoon sea salt

¼ cup Jun Tea (page 75)

1 teaspoon ground cumin

⅛ teaspoon ground cayenne or ground chipotle
    powder

Good water, as needed: well, spring, or filtered

Prepare beans:

1. If using raw beans: Soak beans overnight in water. The next day, drain the beans.

2. Cook with fresh water for a few hours, until soft. Drain the beans.

3. Place beans in a food processor or high speed blender. Add in the remaining ingredients and blend mixture until smooth. If the mixture is too stiff, add a bit more lemon juice or Jun Tea. The mixture should be thick yet creamy. If it is still too pasty, add a bit more water until it's nice and creamy.

4. Scrape mixture into 2 wide mouth pint jars.

5. Seal jars with stainless steel Mason lids. Cover jars with a natural cloth.

6. Ferment at room temperature for 2 to 3 days. Transfer to the refrigerator. Use within a month.

VIVA CHIMICHURRI

Chimichurri is a South American sauce used as a condiment and for marinades. It is usually prepared raw, but fermenting elevates its flavor and nutrition. The probiotic bacteria tenderize meats, aiding their digestion. This recipe can be adapted to use any fresh herbs, such as basil, oregano, arugula, etc. Lacto-fermented herbs make wonderful bases for sauces, dips, marinades, and chutneys. Non-fermented substitutes are included in the recipe.

MAKES: 1 PINT

INGREDIENTS:

2 bunches fresh cilantro

1 bunch flat leaf parsley

2 tablespoons Raw Pickled Garlic (page 39) (or 6 cloves raw garlic)

¼ cup Live-Fermented Onions (page 35) (or 1 medium onion)

2 tablespoons Raw Apple Cider Vinegar (page 89) (or red wine vinegar)

1 tablespoon Raw Pickled Peppers (page 41) or Live-Fermented Hot Sauce (page 43)

Juice from half a lemon—use real, fresh lemon

½ cup good water: well, spring, or filtered

1 teaspoon finely ground sea salt

1 teaspoon freshly ground black pepper

Extra virgin olive oil

Optional:

A pinch of sweetener to taste

1. Remove the large herb stems. Chop herb leaves finely.

2. Place the chopped herbs in a bowl with the remaining ingredients—all *except* the oil. Sprinkle with salt. Stir the mixture well for several minutes.

3. Leave for 30 minutes, stirring occasionally, until the mixture releases natural juices.

4. Pack ingredients into a wide mouth pint Mason jar.

5. Seal with a fermentation lid. Cover the jar with a natural cloth and store in a dark spot at room temperature.

6. Leave the jars to ferment for about 1 week. Check every few days to make sure things are brewing nicely. The paste will develop a slight effervescence, smell slightly sour, and taste tangy.

7. After a week, transfer the paste into a blender or food processor. Pulse the mixture until it becomes a rough paste with some remaining chunks. Transfer to a jar and store in the refrigerator.

8. To serve: bring Chimichurri to room temperature and add olive oil. Chimichurri keeps well for several weeks.

LIVE-FERMENTED GAZPACHO

Gazpacho is a Spanish tomato-based raw vegetable soup, like a "liquid salad." It is a nutritional powerhouse packed with veggies, herbs, and flavored with vinegar and olive oil. This recipe is thick and hearty; for a thinner base, add the optional tomato sauce. Use fresh raw ingredients when live-fermented are unavailable.

MAKES: 1 QUART OR 4 (8-OUNCE) SERVINGS
(IF USING TOMATO SAUCE, IT MAKES ABOUT ½ GALLON)

INGREDIENTS:

12 medium tomatoes (or 2 cups Live-Fermented Tomatoes, page 53)

2 large cucumbers

2 peppers (or ½ cup Raw Pickled Peppers, page 41)

1 red onion (or ½ cup Live-Fermented Onions, page 35)

2 tablespoons Raw Pickled Garlic (page 39) (or 6 cloves raw garlic)

1 cup fresh herbs such as cilantro, basil, parsley, or chives

¼ cup Raw Apple Cider Vinegar (page 89) or Jun Tea (page 75)

Fresh juice of 1 lime

Hot sauce to taste (Live-Fermented Hot Sauce, page 43, if available)

Finely ground sea salt and freshly ground black pepper to taste

¼ cup good quality olive oil

Optional:

1–2 cups Fermented Tomato Sauce (page 53)

¼ cup Pureed SCOBY (page 79)

1. Prepare fresh produce: Peel and dice cucumbers. Dice tomatoes, peppers, and onions. Mince garlic and finely chop herbs.

2. Place everything in a large bowl *except* the olive oil. Combine well. For a smoother gazpacho, puree part or all of the mixture.

3. Place the mixture into a wide mouth quart Mason jar (or 2 quart-size jars, if adding tomato sauce).

4. Seal with a fermentation lid(s). Cover the jar(s) with a natural cloth and store at room temperature.

5. Leave the jars to ferment for 2 days. The high acid in the tomatoes should keep your microbiome environment in check. After 2 days, remove the fermentation lids and replace with stainless steel lids. Store the jars in a refrigerator.

6. Serve chilled. Garnish soup with sauerkraut, pickled peppers, fermented onions, or any other fermented veggie, and sour cream. Fermented Gazpacho keeps well for months.

GARDEN CHILI

In this recipe, the fermented ingredients are cooked and therefore loose some nutritional value, but the fermentation adds an elusive flavor, umami—earthy, meaty, and satisfying. If fermented veggies are unavailable, raw veggies are acceptable. For the sake of ease, canned beans are used; but cooking dried beans from scratch is always welcome.

MAKES: 6 (12-OUNCE) SERVINGS

INGREDIENTS:

½ cup olive oil

1 cup Live-Fermented Onions (page 35)

1 cup Raw Pickled Peppers (page 41)

1 pint Live-Fermented Tomatoes (page 53) or canned tomatoes

2 tablespoons Raw Pickled Garlic (page 39)

2 ounces good quality dark chocolate

2 tablespoons chili powder

2 tablespoons paprika

1 tablespoon whole fennel seeds

1 tablespoon whole cumin seeds

1–2 pieces whole star anise

2 bay leaves

2 tablespoons bouillon or soup base

¼ cup Raw Apple Cider Vinegar (page 89), Jun Tea (page 75), or Pureed SCOBY (page 79)

2 cans any beans, drained

Live-Fermented Hot Sauce (page 43), to taste

Sea salt and freshly ground black pepper to taste

Optional:

½ cup cashews or other nuts

1 pound ground beef, sausage, or other meat

1 cup fermented veggies: Live-Fermented Carrots (page 37), Live-Fermented Turnips (page 54), Live-Fermented Sauerkraut (page 30), etc.

1. Grind the whole spices (except the bay leaves). Set aside.

2. Gently sauté the veggies in olive oil for a few minutes. Fermented veggies are juicy, so they will not caramelize as in traditional sautéing. If using meat, sauté with the veggies.

3. Add spices, tomato, beans, and remaining optional ingredients.

4. Gently bring chili to *just* a boil, and then quickly reduce to a simmer.

5. Simmer on low for about 60 minutes.

6. Taste and adjust flavor with salt and pepper.

7. Serve with more fermented veggies, chopped fresh herbs, and sour cream.

Tip: Chili tastes better if you let it sit overnight in the refrigerator and then reheat it before serving.

RAW PICKLED EGG SALAD

Egg salad is one of those convenient comfort foods that most people love, including children. Pickled egg salad is crunchy, tangy, and bursting with nutrition. Eggs are incredibly nutritious, rich in protein, B-vitamins, and vitamin D. They are heart-healthy sources of unsaturated fats and the "good" cholesterol. This recipe also makes the zippiest live-fermented deviled eggs. Make picnics probiotic!

MAKES: 1 QUART

INGREDIENTS:

12 hard-boiled eggs

¼ cup Live-Fermented Onions (page 35)
(or raw onion)

1 tablespoon Raw Pickled Garlic (page 39)
(or 3 cloves raw garlic)

2–4 tablespoons mayonnaise

1 tablespoon mustard

2 tablespoons Raw Apple Cider Vinegar (page 89)
or Jun Tea (page 75)

2 tablespoons olive oil

½ teaspoon cayenne

Sea salt and freshly ground black pepper

Handful of fresh herbs

Optional:

¼ cup chopped raw pickles, sauerkraut, or turnips

Step 1. Hard-boil the eggs:

1. Place eggs in a pot, cover with water, and sprinkle in sea salt. Bring to a boil, reduce the heat a bit, and boil for 5 to 7 minutes.

2. Remove from the heat, pour off the water, and fill the pot with cold water.

3. Let the eggs cool thoroughly.

Step 2. Make the egg salad:

4. Peel and dice the hardboiled eggs. Roughly chop the herbs (and raw onion and garlic, if using).

5. Sprinkle the chopped herbs, onions, and optional veggies over the eggs.

6. Mix the remaining "sauce" ingredients in a separate bowl.

7. After this sauce is mixed together, gently pour over the egg/veggies. Gently stir everything all together. Adjust the seasoning with salt and pepper, to desired taste. Egg salad tastes better when chilled for at least an hour. It keeps well for about a week.

RAW PICKLED POTATO SALAD

This probiotic potato salad is a delicious way to feature raw pickled vegetables. Potatoes are prebiotic—rich in soluble fibers that feed the gut's microbiome. You can substitute turnips, rutabagas, or any root vegetable for the potatoes.

MAKES: 1 QUART

INGREDIENTS:

2 pounds potatoes: New red or Yukon gold varieties are preferable

1 cup pickle juice

½ cup Live-Fermented Pickles (page 32)

½ cup Live-Fermented Onions (page 35) (or 1 raw onion)

½ cup diced celery

Handful of fresh herbs: parsley, cilantro, fennel, basil, oregano, thyme, etc., or any combination

Marinade:

¼ cup Raw Apple Cider Vinegar (page 89) or Jun Tea (page 75)

2 tablespoons mustard, ideally Dijon

¼ cup olive oil or mayonnaise

2 tablespoons Raw Pickled Garlic (page 39) (or 6 cloves raw garlic)

Sea salt and freshly ground black pepper to taste

1. Rinse the potatoes, leaving skins on. Dice into desired-sized chunks.

2. Place the potatoes and pickle juice in a stockpot. Cover the potatoes with cold water.

3. Cook on medium high, bringing potatoes slowly to a boil. *Just* when they reach a boil, lower the heat immediately to a low-medium temperature and *gently* simmer the potatoes.

4. Cook for about 10 to 15 minutes, until the potatoes feel tender when pierced with a knife. Drain the water and allow the potatoes to cool in a big bowl.

5. Combine all the marinade ingredients together. Set aside.

6. Dice the pickles and onion (if using raw). Finely chop the herbs. Sprinkle the pickles, onions, celery, and herbs over the potatoes.

7. Add marinade to the bowl. Stir gently to combine everything thoroughly. Adjust flavor with sea salt and pepper to desired taste. Potato salad is better when it rests in the refrigerator for a few hours or overnight, allowing the flavors to "marry together."

JUN SOURDOUGH BREAD

As an alternative to traditional sourdough breads, Jun Sourdough uses Jun Tea and SCOBY to enhance the rise and improve the texture. This bread is chewy and moist with a firm crust. It's great for toast, sandwiches, French toast, and soup dipping. As with most of these recipes using ferments, there are many options and substitutions, depending on which ingredients you have on hand.

MAKES: 1 (5" × 9") LOAF

INGREDIENTS:

½ cup good water: well, spring, or filtered, warmed (body temperature)

1 tablespoon sweetener of choice

2 teaspoons yeast

½ cup Jun Tea (page 75) or other fermented beverage

½ cup Pureed SCOBY* (page 79)

1 tablespoon oil or melted butter

1½ teaspoon finely ground sea salt

3 cups all-purpose flour or flours of choice

Optional (use one or some):

½ cup chopped nuts or seeds

½ cup fermented or chopped dried fruits

½ cup cooked whole grains

¼ cup Live-Fermented Onions (page 35) and/or Raw Pickled Garlic (page 39)

Savory spices: caraway, dill, or fennel seeds; onion or garlic powder

Sweet spices: cinnamon; lemon zest; almond extract

*Substitute yogurt or kefir for pureed SCOBY

1. Mix water, sweetener, and yeast in a large bowl and let sit for 5 to 10 minutes. This allows the yeast to "bloom"—awaken and reproduce—which helps the bread rise.

2. Add the remaining ingredients (including optional) and stir slowly for several minutes, until the mixture is smooth. The dough will be sticky and wet.

3. Transfer the dough onto a well-floured board or counter. Using a wooden or plastic dough scraper helps to keep hands clean and dough on the counter.

4. Knead for 10 minutes, adding sprinkles of flour to keep the dough from sticking to hands and counter. Be careful when adding flour, mixing just enough to prevent sticking. Or use a standing mixer with a dough hook to knead the dough.

5. After 10 to 15 minutes of kneading, the dough should still be wet and sticky but now more elastic and stretchy. The texture should feel like a sticky water balloon.

(Continued on next page . . .)

6. Shape into a ball. Grease the mixing bowl and place the dough ball into the bowl.

7. Cover loosely with a natural cloth and place in a warm spot. Let the dough rise until it doubles in size, usually a few hours. When doubled, scrape the dough back onto the lightly floured counter and punch down the dough.

8. Shape the dough: first, flatten the dough. Starting on one end, begin to roll the dough from one end to the other into an oval shape. Keep rolling the dough tightly to avoid big holes baked in the bread.

9. Place the loaf seam-side down into a well-oiled loaf pan.

10. Let rise until the loaf rises just above the top of the loaf pan—45 to 60 minutes. Note: The bread continues to rise in the oven, so avoid the temptation to let it over-rise.

11. While the dough is rising again, prepare the oven: place a pan of water in the bottom of the oven (no plastic handles!). Place a rack in the middle of the oven. Preheat the oven to 450°F.

12. When the loaf has risen, place in the oven and bake for 10 minutes. After 10 minutes, reduce the temperature to 350°F.

13. Open the oven and create steam:. Using a long wooden spoon or spatula, splash water carefully from the water pan creating a steam room environment, and close quickly to trap the steam inside.

14. Bake for another 30 to 40 minutes.

15. Test the bread by turning it out of the pan and patting the loaf's bottom. The sound should be hollow, like a drum. If the bread sticks to the pan's sides, gently separate it with a knife before attempting to remove the bread from the pan.

16. Cool the bread on a wire rack. Let the bread cool thoroughly—at least 2 hours—before slicing.

17. To store, wrap bread in cloth or beeswax wrap. Keep on the counter or in a breadbox. (Refrigerating bread dries it out.)

Notes on flour: A good rule is to use half wheat-based and half "other." Use a variety of flours, such as white, bread flour, wheat, rye, barley, or any grain. King Arthur flours are excellent. They contain no bleach, bromate, or artificial preservatives. For gluten-free options, use buckwheat and gluten-free oat flours. Also try unique flours, such as amaranth and millet.

Notes on yeast: Omit the yeast for a natural wild fermentation version of this bread. The first rise will take longer—several hours or overnight. The second rise may take a few hours. The results will be denser, chewier bread, like a pumpernickel or sourdough rye.

Most people are aware that sourdough bread has less gluten than bread made with baker's yeast, but this isn't the only advantage. Fermentation breaks down phytic acid, increasing the availability of nutrients in the bread. It also produces prebiotics within the bread that feed the good bacteria in our digestive tract. The acidic environment created by fermentation also gives sourdough a longer shelf life than standard bread. (Lau et al, 2021)

SAUERKRAUT FOCACCIA

Focaccia is simple flat bread, friendly for beginners. Think pizza dough meets airy sourdough roll. The optional toppings are a starting point. Try any topping that you enjoy on pizza. Or slice in half for a chewy bun.

MAKES: 2 LOAVES

INGREDIENTS:

2 cups good water: well, spring, or filtered, warmed to body temperature

1 tablespoon raw honey or sweetener of choice

1 rounded tablespoon active dry yeast

2 cups Live-Fermented Sauerkraut (page 30) with the juice*

¼ cup olive oil

5 cups white all-purpose flour OR a combination or white and wheat flour, divided

Optional toppings (one, some, or all):

Herb or spice seeds: caraway, dill, poppy, cumin, etc.

Sesame seeds

Raw Pickled Garlic (page 39), Live-Fermented Onions (page 147), Raw Pickled Peppers (page 41), or Live-Fermented Tomatoes (page 53)

Shredded cheese

*Substitute for sauerkraut other fermented veggies: turnips, carrots, zucchini, etc.

1. Set a rack in the middle of the oven and preheat to 400°F.

2. Line two baking trays with parchment paper or silicone sheets and oil generously.

3. Combine the water, sweetener, and yeast into a large "non-reactive" bowl—glass, stainless steel, or ceramic. Let the mixture sit for a few minutes, allowing the yeast to "bloom." Then add the sauerkraut/juice, olive oil, and half the flour.

4. Stir with a sturdy wooden spoon until the ingredients come together.

5. Slowly add the remaining flour until the dough is soft and sticky, yet holds its shape. Adjust with more flour or water, if necessary.

6. With wet hands, pat the dough and shape into a ball and grease the top with olive oil.

7. Cover the bowl with parchment paper or a natural cloth and place in a warm spot.

8. Let the dough rise and double in size— about 2 to 4 hours.

9. Punch the dough to remove the expanded air, and then "pour" the dough onto the pans.

10. With oily hands, pat into 2 (1-inch-thick) flat crusts, spread over the pan.

11. Sprinkle optional toppings on top.

12. Bake 15 minutes or until puffed and golden. For crispier focaccia, bake 5 minutes more.

13. If the toppings become too dark, lay a piece of parchment paper over the focaccia.

Note: Focaccia dough may cold-ferment in the refrigerator overnight or even for a few days. If cold-fermenting, rest the dough at room temperature for at least 1 hour before pouring the dough into the pans.

GINGER BUG GINGERBREAD

Gingerbread is a "sleeper"—something wonderful yet under-appreciated. Gingerbread is often taken for granted, ho-hum. But it is moist, fragrant, delicious, hearty, and simple. It's also a satisfying breakfast and snack. Adding live-fermented ingredients heightens the flavor, so enjoy in good health!

MAKES: 1 LOAF

DRY INGREDIENTS:

2 cups of all-purpose flour or flour of choice

2 teaspoons ground ginger

½ teaspoon finely ground black pepper

1 teaspoon baking soda

½ teaspoon baking powder

½ teaspoon salt

WET INGREDIENTS:

½ cup oil

1 cup Sucanat or other unrefined sugar*

2 large eggs, room temperature

½ cup Ginger Bug (page 85) or Jun Tea (page 75)

½ cup creamy fermented liquid of choice**: Sweet Potato Fly (page 97), Nut Milk (page 101), Live-Fermented Horchata (page 99), etc.

1 tablespoon grated fresh ginger root

Optional:

½ cup chopped walnuts, dates, chocolate chips, or candied ginger

*Coconut, palm or date sugar, honey, or maple syrup

**Substitute with fermented dairy: yogurt, kefir, or sour cream

1. Place a rack in the middle of the oven. Preheat the oven to 350°F.

2. Line a 9" × 5" loaf pan with parchment paper and lightly grease the paper and pan.

3. Combine dry ingredients in a bowl. Stir or whisk well to remove any lumps.

4. In a larger bowl, whisk together all the wet ingredients, including ginger root.

5. Add dry ingredients into wet, plus any optional ingredients. Stir gently with a sturdy spoon until everything is *just* combined. Resist over-mixing.

6. Pour batter into the loaf pan.

7. Bake for 50 to 60 minutes, rotating the cake halfway through baking.

8. If the top browns too quickly, gently cover with parchment paper or foil. The cake is ready when a toothpick inserted in the middle comes out with a few crumbs.

9. Let gingerbread cool for 15 minutes before removing from the loaf pan. Cool thoroughly before wrapping. This cake keeps well wrapped at room temperature. The ginger flavor develops more after 24 hours.

CULTURED MUFFINS

Here is a basic muffin recipe with a moist and crumby texture. Feel free to add optional ingredients, such as fruits, nuts, seeds, chocolate chips, etc. Or go for savory flavor with cheeses, spinach, onions, etc. This recipe can also be used to make pancakes or quick bread. There are substitutions for most ingredients. These muffins freeze well and also keep fresh for several days on the counter when wrapped well.

MAKES: 12 REGULAR MUFFINS; 6 LARGE MUFFINS; 2 (9" × 5") LOAF PANS; OR 12 PANCAKES

INGREDIENTS:

2 cups all-purpose flour or flour of choice

2 teaspoons baking powder

1 cup fermented beverage of choice:
   Nut Milk (page 101), Sweet Potato Fly (page 97), Bread Kvass (page 103), etc.

½ cup sugar*

¼ cup oil**

1 egg (or vegan egg substitute)

1 teaspoon pure vanilla

Optional (use one or more):

1 teaspoon cinnamon

¼ teaspoon nutmeg, allspice, coriander, and/or cloves

1 tablespoon Ginger Bug (page 85)

½ cup any fermented fruit or sweet veggies: Alive Applesauce (page 108), Blueberries in Honey (page 67), Banana Smash (page 109), Fruit Compote (page 111), Live-Fermented Jam (page 103), Live-Fermented Carrots (page 37), Live-Fermented Sweet Potatoes (page 47), etc.

½ cup raisins, crushed walnuts, shredded coconut, etc.

*Healthy options: Sucanat, coconut palm or date sugar, honey, or maple syrup

**Substitute with applesauce or any fermented dairy product

1. Preheat oven to 350°F and place a rack in the middle of the oven.

2. Line a muffin tin with paper liners or grease well.

3. Whisk the flour, baking powder, and optional dry spices in a bowl. Set aside.

4. In a larger bowl, combine the remaining (wet) ingredients.

5. Add the dry ingredients, plus any other optional ingredients, and stir everything until *just* combined. Resist over-mixing!

6. Spoon into the prepared muffin tins. Fill almost to the top.

7. Bake about 20 minutes, rotating the tray halfway through.

8. Muffins are done when an inserted toothpick comes out clean.

9. Let muffins rest for 10 minutes in their baking tins. Then remove and cool on a wire rack.

Note: If muffins sit loosely covered overnight, their paper liners peel off more easily.

CHOCOLATE SAUERKRAUT CAKE

Sauerkraut cake came about in America in the 1960s. The USDA Surplus Committee challenged school lunchroom managers with a project: come up with ideas to utilize the large quantity of stockpiled canned sauerkraut. This delightful creation is the marriage of Chocolate Cake and Salted Caramel. Experiment with other live-fermented veggies, too!

MAKES: 1 (9" × 13") PAN

DRY INGREDIENTS:

2 cups all-purpose flour or flour of choice

½ cup unsweetened cocoa, Dutch-process or natural

1 teaspoon baking soda

WET INGREDIENTS:

2 cups sugar*

1 cup oil

2 large eggs

1 cup hot water

½ cup fermented liquid of choice: Jun Tea (page 75), Sweet Potato Fly (page 97), Nut Milk (page 101), Bread Kvass (page 103), etc.

1 teaspoon pure vanilla

1 cup Live-Fermented Sauerkraut (page 30)**

Optional:

½ cup nuts, chocolate chips, coconut, etc.

*Healthy options: Sucanat; coconut palm or date sugar; honey or maple syrup

**Substitute with shredded turnips, carrots, sweet potatoes, zucchini, beets, etc.

1. An hour or two before beginning, place eggs on counter to bring to room temperature.

2. Drain sauerkraut into a bowl, reserving the liquid.

3. Place the wire rack in the middle of the oven and pre-heat oven to 350°F.

4. Grease and flour 9" × 13" cake or Bundt pan.

5. Pat sauerkraut to remove moisture and chop finely.

6. Place the dry ingredients in a bowl. Whisk together until fully combined and lump-free.

7. In a larger bowl, add the wet ingredients (sugar included), and whisk together well.

8. Add dry ingredients into wet ingredients. Mix gently and thoroughly.

9. Pour into cake pan and bake for about 30 minutes. Rotate pan halfway through cooking.

10. Cake is ready when a few moist crumbs stick to an inserted toothpick. Note: It's better to under-bake chocolate baked goods! They dry out when cooling.

11. Let cake rest for about 10 minutes in the pan, then turn out onto a wire cooling rack. Allow cake to fully cool before eating.

Serving suggestions: sprinkle with confectioner's sugar; top with chocolate glaze or fruit; serve with whipped or ice cream.

TAHINI COOKIES

Tahini is a perfect baking ingredient. It works like both oil and egg, and it is allergy-friendly. Tahini keeps cookies moist for days! Crisp on the edges and cakelike in the middle, these sweeties have all the things you want in a cookie.

MAKES: 2 DOZEN

DRY INGREDIENTS:

½ cup all-purpose flour or flour of choice

1 teaspoon baking soda

½ teaspoon finely ground sea salt

WET INGREDIENTS:

1 cup Sucanat or other unrefined sugar*

1 cup tahini**

1 egg

1 tablespoon Raw Apple Cider Vinegar (page 89) or other fermented liquid of choice

1 teaspoon pure vanilla

Optional:

½ cup sesame seeds, set aside

1 teaspoon cinnamon, ginger, or cardamom

½ cup chocolate chips or shredded coconut

2 tablespoons Pureed SCOBY (page 79) (makes a spongier cookie)

*Coconut, palm, or date sugars are best. Brown sugar is acceptable.

**Substitute with any nut butter

1. An hour or two before beginning, remove eggs and tahini from the refrigerator. Stir tahini well.

2. When ready to begin, stagger two racks in the middle of the oven. Preheat oven to 350°F.

3. Line two cookie sheets with parchment paper or Silpat/silicone sheets.

4. Combine dry ingredients in a bowl. Stir or whisk well to remove any lumps.

5. In a larger bowl, whisk together the wet ingredients. Add dry ingredients (and optional ingredients) to wet ingredients. Stir gently until fully combined.

6. Chill dough for at least 2 hours. This cookie dough is good chilled up to a few days.

7. After chilling, scoop the dough with a large spoon and roll into balls.

8. If using sesame seeds: Drop balls into the bowl of sesame seeds, pressing gently to flatten cookies slightly.

9. These cookies spread as they bake, so place up to 12 cookies on each regular baking tray.

10. Bake for 10 to 12 minutes, rotating the tray halfway through baking.

11. Bake them until they are soft to the touch—slightly underdone. Place on a cooling rack.

12. Let cookies cool for about 10 minutes, and then transfer onto a wire cooling rack. Store at room temperature. Cookies keep well for several days.

FRUIT LEATHER

Fermented foods should be a daily part of every whole food diet, even for children. Getting kids to enjoy fermented foods might be difficult for parents. To introduce them to this new world, fruit leather is the answer: kid-friendly taste with gut-friendly probiotics. Fruit leather keeps everyone happy!

MAKES: 2-3 POUNDS

INGREDIENTS:

2–3 pounds of fruit

¼ cup fruity fermented beverage: Fruit Scrap Soda (page 83), Fizzy Lemonade (page 87), or Jun Tea (page 75)

Sweetener to taste

Spices to taste

Optional:

¼ cup Pureed SCOBY (page 79)

1. Gently rinse and dry fruit. Remove cores, pits, and seeds, and cut into small pieces.

2. Puree the fruit in a blender or food processor until smooth.

3. Add the spices, sweetener, and about 1 to 2 tablespoons fermented beverage. Pulse/mix to combine until it has a spreadable paste consistency. Add more fermented beverage or pureed SCOBY if the mixture is too thick.

4. Transfer to a wide mouth quart Mason jar, leaving an inch of space at the top.

5. Seal with a fermentation lid. Cover the jar with a natural cloth and store in a dark spot at room temperature.

6. Leave to ferment for about 3 days. Check the fruit mixture every day. It develops a slight effervescence and smells tangy.

7. After 3 days, spread the cultured fruit mixture onto sheets of unbleached parchment paper or a Silpat/silicon sheet. The fruited sheets should fit on a baking tray or in a food dehydrator, if you are using one.

8. Set the oven temperature to warm or about 110°F in a food dehydrator.

9. Dry the paste between 8 to 24 hours. The length of time depends on several factors: thickness of the mixture, temperature of the oven, and type of food dehydrator. The type of fruit used also affects drying time, as some fruits dry more slowly. If needed, dry the leather for an additional day. Fruit leather is done when it peels easily off the drying sheet. Store the finished fruit leather in an airtight container.

Note: If drying in the oven, turn the oven off at night. The dehydrator may remain on.

If the mixture seems watery after fermenting, strain out the excess juice through a coffee filter or cheesecloth. Save and enjoy this bubbly juice as a sweet healthy elixir!

JUN-AIGRETTE

Jun-aigrette is a healthier version of vinaigrette. Here's a basic live-fermented salad dressing that can be adapted so many ways by adding different herbs and spices. It makes a great marinade, too!

Olive oil improves heart health and brain function. Jun tea is an immune stimulant. Garlic's natural antibiotic, anti-viral, anti-fungal properties are legendary. Black pepper helps treat respiratory disorders. Food is medicine!

MAKES: 1 PINT

INGREDIENTS:

½ cup Jun Tea (page 75)*

1 cup olive oil—organic, extra virgin, cold pressed preferably

2 tablespoons good water: well, spring, or filtered

1 tablespoon Raw Pickled Garlic (page 39)

1 tablespoon raw honey or maple syrup

1 tablespoon mustard, Dijon preferably

Sea salt and freshly ground black pepper to taste

Optional:

¼ cup fresh herbs or Live-Fermented Greens (page 59)

2 tablespoons Live-Fermented Onions (page 35)

2 teaspoons Raw Pickled Peppers (page 41) or Live-Fermented Hot Sauce (page 43)

2 tablespoons Pureed SCOBY (page 79), for a creamier texture

*Replace half or all Jun Tea with Raw Apple Cider Vinegar (page 89) for a tangier dressing.

1. Place all ingredients into a blender. Blend at low, then high speed.

2. Store in the refrigerator. Jun-aigrette stays well for months.

Cruciferous vegetables are high in sulfur-containing compounds. This is what gives them their strong smell and taste. One of these compounds, sulforaphane, has been found to be very strongly antioxidant and anti-inflammatory. Health conditions it has been shown to benefit include autism spectrum disorder, cancer, and type 2 diabetes. It even helps the body eliminate toxins from air pollution. Foods high in sulforaphane include cabbage, broccoli, brussels sprouts, and greens such as kale, collards, and mustard greens.

LIVE-FERMENTED BARBEQUE SAUCE

Ribs, pulled pork, fries . . . delicious yes, but they are gut bombs. Let's make the whole barbeque experience healthier . . . with a gut balm! This live-fermented sauce helps break down the heavy load of protein, easing digestion. Plus, it adds that unique umami flavor that only a fermented food can offer. Giddy up!

MAKES: 1 PINT

INGREDIENTS:

1 cup fermented or dried fruit: apples, apricots, prunes, raisins, etc.

1 cup good water: well, spring, or filtered

½ cup Beet or Bread Kvass (page 93 or 103), or any other fermented beverage

¼ cup mustard

¼ cup Live-Fermented Onions (page 35) (or 1 medium raw onion)

2 teaspoons Raw Pickled Garlic (page 39) (or 4 raw garlic cloves)

¼ cup maple syrup, raw honey, or molasses

Sea salt and freshly ground black pepper to taste

Optional:

1 tablespoon smoked paprika

2 tablespoons bourbon

1 tablespoon Live-Fermented Hot Sauce (page 43)

1. If using dried fruit: Soak the fruit in water overnight. The next day, drain the fruit. (Save the water, in case the sauce needs thinning.)

2. Combine all the ingredients into a blender or food processor.

3. Blend on low, then medium, and then low again, until smooth. This takes 1 to 2 minutes.

4. Adjust consistency with more fermented beverage or the leftover fruit-water.

5. Adjust flavor with salt and pepper. Add optional herbs to desired taste.

6. Store in the refrigerator. Keeps well for about a month.

Note: The barbeque sauce will cold-ferment, so taste periodically. If it becomes too sour, add more sweetener or use as a marinade. Or add it to your next batch of chili.

FERMENTED PET TREATS: SCOBY DOOS

SCOBYs are incredibly versatile. They add texture to bread, fortify smoothies, thicken jams, etc. SCOBYs have even been used as faux leather in clothing. Dehydrated, they become wonderful healthy pet treats. Woof! Meow!

MAKES: ABOUT 1 POUND OF TREATS

INGREDIENTS:

2 cups whole Jun SCOBYs
  (about 2 inches of SCOBYs)

Gluconic acid is one of the compounds formed by fermentation. It easily bonds to minerals such as calcium, zinc, copper, iron, and potassium, and serves as an excellent delivery system for those minerals. Any supplement with gluconate in the name is this type of compound.

1. Cut up the SCOBYs into strips or chunks.

2. Dry one of several ways: Place them in a food dehydrator set to 95°F OR place on a sheet tray in an oven set to the warm setting OR sun-dry on a sheet tray covered with a screen or cheesecloth. Dehydrate for several hours until thoroughly dry.

3. SCOBY Doos can be stored for several months in a sealed container. If the treats are still a bit moist, store them in the refrigerator. Moist treats are good for about a month. Discard if they grow mold.

FERMENTED BODY CARE PRODUCTS

These skincare recipes were designed with basic pantry staples in mind. Ingredients are easily accessible from a backyard, farmers market, natural food store, or most supermarkets. Some recipes could include light foraging skills like collecting weeds, pine needles, juniper berries, etc.

A note of caution with foraging: Even though these are common plants, *always* correctly identify plants for the first time with an experienced forager.

SKINAIGRETTE

Skinaigrette is a completely edible, live-fermented body lotion. It's basically vinaigrette—salad dressing or marinade made with oil and acid. Most DIY lotions contain emulsifiers like beeswax to avoid separation. Vinegar and aloe vera are slightly emulsifying, so shaking the bottle or storing in the refrigerator should keep it creamy.

To fully emulsify the lotion for a creamy texture, the recipe uses a special ingredient called glucomannan *or konjac root, a food thickener with medicinal properties. Konjac is used to lower cholesterol and for weight loss. Konjac emulsifies or bonds with fats, whether it's in our bodies or in this lotion.*

MAKES: 1 PINT

INGREDIENTS:

¼ cup coconut oil

¼ cup olive oil

¼ cup Raw Apple Cider Vinegar (page 89)

½ cup good water: well, spring, or filtered

¼ cup aloe vera gel

Several drops of lemon essential oil*

Optional for extra emulsion and creaminess:

1 teaspoon *glucomannan* powder (konjac root)

Extra water, as needed

*Try peppermint, orange, thyme, almond, etc. **Food-grade** essential oils are preferable, as they are produced in safer ways and may be gentler on the skin.

1. Blend all ingredients on low, then high, for about 60 seconds total.

2. Transfer into a glass jar and seal.

3. Apply generously anywhere on the body. Rub in well. Use regularly on brown spots or skin issues. Lotion lasts for a few weeks in the cupboard or several months in the refrigerator.

Note: If Skinaigrette becomes too firm in the refrigerator, it can be stored at room temperature. However, if left out, it may separate like a salad dressing (vinaigrette). If leaving out, store in a lotion-type bottle with a squirt lid. To apply, shake well and then squirt slowly, rubbing in well.

SCOBY BODY SCRUB

With its probiotic enzymatic riches, SCOBY is a wonderful healing remedy for many skin ailments, including acne, psoriasis, rosacea, dermatitis, eczema, cuts, burns, scrapes, and even helping to heal baby's cradle cap. Combining SCOBY with sugar and oats creates a gentle exfoliate, soothing yet thoroughly cleansing.

MAKES: 1 PINT

INGREDIENTS:

½ cup unrefined sugar—Sucanat, coconut, date, or palm sugar

2 tablespoons olive or coconut oil

1 cup organic rolled oats

½ cup Pureed SCOBY (page 79)

2 tablespoons Jun Tea (page 75) or Raw Apple Cider Vinegar (page 89)

1. If using coconut oil: melt and cool slightly.

2. Grind the rolled oats in a high-speed blender or food processor.

3. Combine all ingredients together in a bowl. Mix well.

4. Transfer to a glass jar and store in the refrigerator.

5. To use, apply generously to the whole body (avoid the eyes) and scrub gently. Rinse well in the shower. Body Scrub keeps well for about 1 month.

Everyone knows that Lactobacillus produce lactic acid, but did you know that there are other ways to benefit from it without drinking it? Lactic acid is one of the most common chemicals used in skin care products because it is a mild alpha hydroxy acid. It exfoliates the skin, stimulates collagen, and promotes the skin to self-moisturize. It's even used in creams for keratosis pilaris (chicken skin). The biggest things to watch out for if you are using it topically are skin sensitivity and increased sensitivity to sunlight.

FERMENTED FACIAL TONER

These last two recipes are contributed by Donica Krebs:

Raw apple cider vinegar has been used for centuries as a curative for hundreds of ailments, especially with skin care. It's effective in removing growths, healing acne, and fading brown spots. These last two recipes call for light foraging skills in collecting fresh yarrow and plantain, both common yard plants. Fresh herbs are always optimal, but dried is acceptable.

MAKES: 1 PINT (16 OUNCES)

INGREDIENTS:

1 cup Raw Apple Cider Vinegar* (page 89)

2 tablespoons rose petals

1 tablespoon fresh yarrow leaf and flower

1 tablespoon fresh plantain leaves

1 cup good water: well, spring, or filtered

*Store-bought apple cider vinegar may be more acidic. Homemade apple cider vinegar seems to be gentler, perhaps having a lower acidity, or from being better quality.

Note: For sensitive skin, add more water if desired.

Caution: *Always* have an experienced forager correctly identify plants the first time.

1. Combine vinegar and herbs in a jar. Cover with a lid and "pickle" for 2 weeks in the refrigerator.

2. Strain the liquid. Add 1 cup water to the floral vinegar and shake gently.

3. Apply toner with a cotton ball or gentle cloth to clean skin, remove dead skin cells, add a probiotic boost to the skin biome, and soothe with restorative herbs. Allow toner to dry, and then apply Skinaigrette. The ACV smell dissipates as the toner and moisturizer dry.

FERMENTED FACIAL MASK

This facial mask recipe is a base that can be easily customized. Oats are calming and hydrating, cabbage (sauerkraut juice) is high in vitamin C (antiaging), honey has antibacterial properties, the probiotic benefits from fermentation can help restore the skin's natural biome, and different herbs can be used to achieve different medicinal results.

MAKES: ABOUT 1 PINT (16 OUNCES)

INGREDIENTS:

1 cup good water: well, spring, or filtered

½ cup organic rolled oats

¼ cup Live-Fermented Sauerkraut (or other live-fermented) juice (page 30)

1 teaspoon raw honey

2 tablespoons fresh or dried herbs

1. Choose one or more of the following herbs, depending on your skin's needs:

   - Dry or irritated skin: yarrow, lavender, chamomile, rose petal
   - Aging skin: parsley, yarrow, rose petal
   - Oily/acne prone skin: oregano, marjoram, rosemary, raw garlic
   - Hormonal acne: red raspberry leaf, alfalfa, yarrow, sage

2. Blend oats until they are a "corn-mealy" texture. Combine all ingredients in a jar.

3. If the mixture ends up being very thick, add some more sauerkraut juice until a thinner consistency is achieved (think of thin pancake batter).

4. Cover with a coffee filter or cloth. Stir daily.

5. Ferment until bubbling has ceased, about 1 to 2 weeks. Store in the refrigerator.

6. Apply paste to clean skin and allow it to dry. Can be used on the face and neck, eczema spots, surgical scars on the body, etc. Remove gently with warm water.

Caution: ALWAYS have an experienced forager correctly identify plants the first time.

RESOURCES

- Menards: https://www.menards.com/main/grocery-home/grocery/canning-supplies/ball-reg-wide-mouth-quart-mason-jars-12-pack/67000/p-1549438232162-c-1462209588021.htm
- Walmart: https://www.walmart.com/ip/Ball-R-Wide-Mouth-Mason-Cannin-Jars-12-Pkg-Quart-32oz/16930173

POUNDER/PACKER & FERMENTATION PUMP:

- Cultures for Health: https://culturesforhealth.com/collections/vegetables/products/pickle-packer-vegetable-tamper
- Sauerstomper: https://humblehouse.co/shop/sauerstomper-sauerkraut-pounder/
- Nourished Essentials: https://nourishedessentials.com/products/the-easy-fermenter
- Roots and Harvest: https://www.rootsandharvest.com/product/cabbage-stomper/fermenting-accessories

LIDS:

- Nourished Essentials: https://nourishedessentials.com/products/the-easy-fermenter
- Cultures for Health: https://culturesforhealth.com/collections/vegetables/products/pickle-pipe-fermentation-airlock-4-pack
- Mason Jar Lifestyle: https://masonjarlifestyle.com/product/stainless-steel-storage-lids-caps-with-silicone-seals-for-mason-jars/
- Roots and Harvest: https://www.rootsandharvest.com/product/pickle-pipe-air-locks/fermenting-accessories

WEIGHTS:

- Cultures for Health: https://culturesforhealth.com/products/pickle-pebbles-4-pack
- Nourished Essentials: https://nourishedessentials.com/products/the-easy-weight-fermentation-weights-with-grooved-handles

- Mason Jar Lifestyle: https://masonjarlifestyle.com/product/glass-fermentation-weights-fermenting-wide-mouth-mason-jars/

FERMENTATION KITS:

- TrueLeaf Market: https://www.trueleafmarket.com/products/stainless-steel-fermenting
- Roots and Harvest: https://www.rootsandharvest.com/product/fermenting-kit-2-liter-crock/fermenting-kits
- Kombucha Kamp: https://www.kombuchakamp.com/jun-tea-brew-now-kit.html
- Happy Herbalist: https://www.happyherbalist.com/jun-starter-kit/
- The Kombucha Shop: https://www.thekombuchashop.com/

CLOTH COVERS:

- King Arthur: https://shop.kingarthurbaking.com/items/king-arthur-flour-sack-towels-set-of-4
- Vermont Country Store: https://www.vermontcountrystore.com/floursack-cotton-towel-sets-in-2-sizes/product/63272

BEESWAX:

- Bee's Wrap: https://www.beeswrap.com/
- King Arthur: https://shop.kingarthurbaking.com/items/bees-wrap-roll

SANITATION:

- Bleach: https://shop.clorox.com/products/clorox-splash-less-bleach1
- Hydrogen Peroxide: https://www.seventhgeneration.com/chlorine-free-bleach

JUN SCOBY:

- Kombucha Kamp: https://www.kombuchakamp.com/jun-culture.html
- Cultures for Health: https://culturesforhealth.com/products/jun-tea-kombucha-starter-culture
- Oregon Kombucha: https://oregonkombucha.com/products/jun-scoby-and-starter-for-homebrewing?variant=17579975934067

SALT:

- Redmond Sea Salt: https://redmond.life/collections/real-salt
- Celtic Sea Salt: https://www.celticseasalt.com/

- SAF: https://shop.kingarthurbaking.com/items/saf-red-instant-yeast
- SAF Information: https://saf-instant.com/en/professional/

FLOUR:

- King Arthur: https://shop.kingarthurbaking.com/flours
- Milestone Mill: https://milestonemill.com/
- Carolina Ground: https://carolinaground.com/

ORGANIZATIONS:

- Sandor Ellix Katz: https://www.wildfermentation.com/
- Ann Wigmore Institute: https://annwigmore.org/

SOURCES

- Bar-On, Y. M., Phillips, R., & Milo, R. (2018). The Biomass Distribution on Earth. *Proceedings of the National Academy of Sciences.*
- Bekar, O., Yilmaz, Y., & Gulten, M. (2011). Kefir improves the efficacy and tolerability of triple therapy in eradicating Helicobacter pylori. *Journal of Medicinal Food*, 14(4), 344–347. https://doi.org/10.1089/jmf.2010.0099
- Jianfen Liang, B.-Z. H. (2008). Effects of soaking, germination and fermentation on phytic acid, total and in vitro soluble zinc in brown rice. *Food Chemistry*, 100 (4), 821-828.
- Kaashyap M, C. M. (2021, Dec 13). Microbial Diversity and Characteristics of Kombucha as Revealed by Metagenomic and Physicochemical Analysis. Retrieved from PubMed Central: https://www.ncbi.nlm.nih.gov/pmc/articles/PMC8704692/
- Lau, Siew Wen et al. "Sourdough Microbiome Comparison and Benefits." Microorganisms vol. 9,7 1355. 23 Jun. 2021, doi:10.3390/microorganisms9071355
- Ousaaid, Driss et al. "Beneficial Effects of Apple Vinegar on Hyperglycemia and Hyperlipidemia in Hypercaloric-Fed Rats." *Journal of Diabetes Research* vol. 2020 9284987. 10 Jul. 2020, doi:10.1155/2020/9284987
- Rosa, D., Dias, M., Grześkowiak, Ł, Reis, S., Conceição, L., & Peluzio, M. (2017). Milk kefir: Nutritional, microbiological and health benefits. Nutrition Research Reviews, 30(1), 82-96.doi:10.1017/S0954422416000275
- Shao, Zhanmei et al. "Effect of Kvass on Improving Functional Dyspepsia in Rats." *Computational and Mathematical Methods in Medicine* vol. 2022 5169892. 28 Jun. 2022, doi:10.1155/2022/5169892
- Tilgner, D. S. (2009). Herbal Medicine From the Heart of the Earth. Wise Acres.
- Zabat MA, S. W. (2018, May 12). Microbial Community Analysis of Sauerkraut Fermentation Reveals a Stable and Rapidly Established Community. Retrieved from PubMed Central: https://www.ncbi.nlm.nih.gov/pmc/articles/PMC5977097/

METRIC CONVERSIONS

If you're accustomed to using metric measurements, use these handy charts to convert the imperial measurements used in this book.

Weight (Dry Ingredients)

1 oz		30 g
4 oz	¼ lb	120 g
8 oz	½ lb	240 g
12 oz	¾ lb	360 g
16 oz	1 lb	480 g
32 oz	2 lb	960 g

Oven Temperatures

Fahrenheit	Celsius	Gas Mark
225°	110°	¼
250°	120°	½
275°	140°	1
300°	150°	2
325°	160°	3
350°	180°	4
375°	190°	5
400°	200°	6
425°	220°	7
450°	230°	8

Volume (Liquid Ingredients)

½ tsp.		2 ml
1 tsp.		5 ml
1 Tbsp.	½ fl oz	15 ml
2 Tbsp.	1 fl oz	30 ml
¼ cup	2 fl oz	60 ml
⅓ cup	3 fl oz	80 ml
½ cup	4 fl oz	120 ml
⅔ cup	5 fl oz	160 ml
¾ cup	6 fl oz	180 ml
1 cup	8 fl oz	240 ml
1 pt	16 fl oz	480 ml
1 qt	32 fl oz	960 ml

Length

¼ in	6 mm
½ in	13 mm
¾ in	19 mm
1 in	25 mm
6 in	15 cm
12 in	30 cm

INDEX

A

apple cider vinegar
  Raw Apple Cider Vinegar, 89
    Banana Smash, 109
    Fermented Facial Toner, 156
    Fizzy Lemonade, 87
    Garden Chili, 125
    Jun-aigrette, 147
    Live-Fermented Hot Sauce, 43
    Live-Fermented Gazpacho, 123
    Raw Pickled Egg Salad, 127
    Raw Pickled Potato Salad, 129
    Raw Pickled Salsa, 117
    SCOBY Body Scrub, 155
    Shrub or Switchel, 91
    Sauerkraut Focaccia, 135
    Skinaigrette, 154
    Sweet Potato Fly, 97
    Tahini Cookies, 143
    Viva Chimichurri, 121
applesauce
  Alive Applesauce, 108
    Cultured Muffins, 139
    Live-Fermented Jam, 113
autoimmune, 11–12

B

bacteria, 1–23, 75
Banana Smash, 109
  Cultured Muffins, 139
barbeque sauce
  Live-Fermented Barbeque Sauce, 149
beets, 22, 31
  Beet Kvass, 93
  Live-Fermented Smoothies, 115

Raw Pickled Beets, 49
  Live-Fermented Smoothies, 115
Blueberries in Honey, 67
  Cultured Muffins, 139
body scrub. See SCOBY body scrub
bread
  Cultured Muffins, 139
  Ginger Bug Gingerbread, 137
  Jun Sourdough Bread, 131–133
  Sauerkraut Focaccia, 135
  Traditional Bread Kvass, 103
brine method, 9, 18–19
  Raw Pickles, 32–33

C

cake. See Chocolate Sauerkraut Cake.
canning, 3
carrots, 19. 31, 125, 135, 141
  Live-Fermented Carrots, 37
    Chocolate Sauerkraut Cake, 141
    Cultured Muffins, 139
    Garden Chili, 125
    Live-Fermented Smoothies, 115
chili
  Garden Chili, 125
chimichurri
  Viva Chimichurri, 121
Chocolate Sauerkraut Cake, 141
cloudy brine, 23–24
cold fermentation, 20
Cold-Fermented Cooler Tea/Tisane, 95
cookies. See Tahini Cookies.
Cultured Muffins, 139

D

dilly beans
Raw Pickled Dilly Beans, 51
dry salt method, 9, 18–19
Live-Fermented Sauerkraut, 30–31
Live-Fermented Greens, 59

E

egg salad
Raw Pickled Egg Salad, 127
enzymes, 5, 10, 14, 24,

F

face care
Fermented Facial Mask, 157
Fermented Facial Toner, 156
"Farm & Forage" Fire Cider, 69
ferment, 1–25
fermentation checklist, 25
Fermented Facial Mask, 157
Fermented Facial Toner, 156
Fermented Hot Honey, 71
Fermented Pet Treats: SCOBY Doos, 151
foraging, 153, 156, 157
Fruit Compote or "Pie-in-a-Jar," 111
Cultured Muffins, 139
Live-Fermented Jam, 113
Live-Fermented Smoothies, 115
Fruit Leather, 145
Fruit Scrap Soda, 83
Alive Applesauce, 108
Fizzy Lemonade, 87
Fruit Leather, 145
Live-Fermented Jam, 113
Fire Cider, 69
Fizzy Lemonade, 87
Alive Applesauce, 108
Banana Smash, 109
Fruit Leather, 145
Live-Fermented Jam, 113
functional foods, 5

G

GABA, 10

Garden Chili, 125
garlic
"Farm & Forage" Fire Cider, 69
Healthier Hummus, 119
Live-Fermented Barbeque Sauce, 149
Live-Fermented Gazpacho, 123
Live-Fermented Greens, 59
Live-Fermented Hot Sauce, 43
Live-Fermented Sauerkraut, 30–31
Live-Fermented Spicy Veggies, 57
Live-Fermented Tomatoes, 53
Raw Pickled Beets, 49
Raw Pickled Egg Salad, 127
Raw Pickled Dilly Beans, 51
Raw Pickled Garlic, 39
Garden Chili, 125
Healthier Hummus, 119
Jun-aigrette, 147
Jun Sourdough Bread, 131–133
Live-Fermented Barbeque Sauce, 149
Sauerkraut Focaccia, 135
Raw Pickled Peppers, 41
Raw Pickled Potato Salad, 129
Raw Pickled Root Vegetables, 55
Raw Pickled Salsa, 117
Raw Pickled Stalks, 61
Raw Pickled Summer Squash, 45
Raw Pickled Watermelon Rind, 65
Raw Pickled Weeds, 63
Raw Pickles, 32–33
Viva Chimichurri, 121
gazpacho, 117
Live-Fermented Gazpacho, 123
Ginger Bug, 85
Alive Applesauce, 108
Cultured Muffins, 139
Fizzy Lemonade, 87
Ginger Bug Gingerbread, 137
Live-Fermented Sweet Potatoes, 47
Second Ferments, 81
Sweet Potato Fly, 97
ginger root, 31, 37, 47, 57, 69, 85, 97, 111, 137

glucomannan. *See* konjac root

gluten, 5, 11, 105, 132

green beans. *See* dilly beans.

green tea, 75–77

greens

    Live-Fermented Greens: *Gundruk*, 59

Gundruk. See greens.

gut, viii–ix, 6, 10–12, 24

gut-brain axis, ix, 10–12

H

horchata

    Live-Fermented Horchata, 99

        Ginger Bug Gingerbread, 137

honey

    Banana Smash, 109

    Blueberries in Honey, 67

    Chocolate Sauerkraut Cake, 141

    Cultured Muffins, 139

    "Farm & Forage" Fire Cider, 69

    Fermented Facial Mask, 157

    Fermented Hot Honey, 71

    Fizzy Lemonade, 87

    Fruit Compote or "Pie-in-a-Jar," 111

    Fruit Scrap Soda, 83

    Ginger Bug, 85

    Gingerbug Gingerbread, 137

    Jun Tea, 75–77

    Jun-aigrette, 147

    Live-Fermented Barbeque Sauce, 149

    Live-Fermented Jam, 113

    Live-Fermented Horchata, 99

    Live-Fermented Smoothies, 115

    Sauerkraut Focaccia, 135

    Second Ferments, 81

    Shrub or Switchel, 91

    Sweet Potato Fly, 97

    Traditional Beet Kvass, 103

hot sauce

    Live-Fermented Hot Sauce, 43

        Garden Chili, 125

        Jun-aigrette, 147

        Live-Fermented Barbeque Sauce, 149

        Live-Fermented Gazpacho, 123

        Raw Pickled Salsa, 117

        Viva Chimchurri, 121

    Healthier Hummus, 119

I

inoculant. *See* starter.

J

jam

    Live-Fermented Jam, 113

        Cultured Muffins, 139

        Live-Fermented Smoothies, 115

Jun

    Jun-aigrette, 147

    Jun Sourdough Bread, 131–133

        Traditional Bread Kvass, 103

    Jun Tea, 75–77

        Alive Applesauce, 108

        Banana Smash, 109

        Chocolate Sauerkraut Cake, 141

        Fizzy Lemonade, 87

        Fruit Compote or "Pie-in-a-Jar," 111

        Fruit Leather, 145

        Garden Chili, 125

        Ginger Bug Gingerbread, 137

        Healthier Hummus, 119

        Live-Fermented Gazpacho, 123

        Live-Fermented Jam, 113

        Jun-aigrette, 147

        Jun Sourdough Bread, 131–133

        Pureed SCOBY, 79

        Raw Pickled Egg Salad, 127

        Raw Pickled Potato Salad, 129

        Raw Pickled Salsa, 117

        SCOBY Body Scrub, 155

        Second Ferments, 81

        Sweet Potato Fly, 97

K

Kahm, 23–24

kimchi, 2

    Live-Fermented Spicy: Kimchi-*ish*, 57

kombucha, 2, 14, 75, 77, 81

konjac root

Skinaigrette, 154
knotweed. *See* weeds.
kvass
  Beet Kvass, 93
  Chocolate Sauerkraut Cake, 141
  Fruit Compote, 111
  Live-Fermented Barbeque Sauce, 149
  Traditional Bread Kvass, 103
  Cultured Muffins, 139

L
Lactobacillus, 9, 12, 23, 75, 155
lacto-fermenting, 9
leaky gut, viii, 11–12
lemonade. *See* Fizzy Lemonade.
Live-Fermented Barbeque Sauce, 149
Live-Fermented Carrots, 37. *See also* carrots.
Live-Fermented Gazpacho, 123
Live-Fermented Greens: *Gundruk*, 59
Live-Fermented Horchata, 99
Live-Fermented Hot Sauce, 43
Live-Fermented Jam, 113
Live-Fermented Onions, 35. *See also* onions.
Live-Fermented Sauerkraut, 30–31. *See also* sauerkraut.
Live-Fermented Smoothies, 115
Live-Fermented Spicy Veggies: Kimchi-*ish*, 57
Live-Fermented Sweet Potatoes, 47. *See also* potatoes.
Live-Fermented Tomatoes/Tomato Sauce, 53. *See also* tomatoes.
Live-Fermented Turnips: *Sauerruben*, 54. *See also* turnips.
lotion. *See* Skinaigrette.

M
magic, 1–2, 9, 20
microbe, 1, 5–6, 10, 15–16, 22, 24
microbiome, ix, 2, 10, 14, 18, 23
muffins. *See* Cultured Muffins.

N
non-reactive equipment, 22, 25
Nut Milk, 101

Chocolate Sauerkraut Cake, 141
Cultured Muffins, 139
Ginger Bug Gingerbread, 137
Live-Fermented Smoothies, 115

O
off-gas, 23, 81
onions, 35
  "Farm & Forage" Fire Cider, 69
  Live-Fermented Barbeque Sauce, 149
  Live-Fermented Gazpacho, 123
  Live-Fermented Greens, 59
  Live-Fermented Hot Sauce, 43
  Live-Fermented Onions, 35
    Garden Chili, 125
    Jun-aigrette, 147
    Jun Sourdough Bread, 131–133
    Sauerkraut Focaccia, 135
  Live-Fermented Sauerkraut, 30–31
  Live-Fermented Sweet Potatoes, 47
  Live-Fermented Spicy Veggies, 57
  Live-Fermented Tomatoes, 53
  Raw Pickled Egg Salad, 127
  Raw Pickled Potato Salad, 129
  Raw Pickled Salsa, 117
  Viva Chimichurri, 121
organic, 15, 18
oxymels, 91

P
pancakes. *See* Cultured Muffins.
pasteurization, 3, 13
pet treats
  Fermented Pet Treats: SCOBY Doos, 151
phytates, 6
peppers
  "Farm & Forage" Fire Cider, 69
  Fermented Hot Honey, 71
  Live-Fermented Greens, 59
  Live-Fermented Hot Sauce, 43
  Live-Fermented Sauerkraut, 30–31
  Live-Fermented Spicy Veggies, 57
  Live-Fermented Tomatoes, 53
  Raw Pickled Peppers, 41

Garden Chili, 125
Jun-aigrette, 147
Live-Fermented Gazpacho, 123
Raw Pickled Salsa, 117
Sauerkraut Focaccia, 135
Viva Chimichurri, 121
Raw Pickled Greens, 63
pickles
Raw Pickled Beets, 49
Raw Pickled Egg Salad, 127
Raw Pickled Dilly Beans, 51
Raw Pickled Garlic, 39
Raw Pickled Peppers, 41
Raw Pickled Potato Salad, 129
Raw Pickled Root Vegetables, 55
Raw Pickled Salsa, 117
Raw Pickled Stalks, 61
Raw Pickled Summer Squash, 45
Raw Pickled Watermelon Rind, 65
Raw Pickled Weeds, 63
Raw Pickles, 32–33
Pie-in-a-Jar. *See* Fruit Compote.
potatoes. *See also* sweet potatoes.
Live-Fermented Sweet Potatoes, 47
Cultured Muffins, 139
Live-Fermented Smoothies, 115
Raw Pickled Potato Salad, 129
Sweet Potato Fly, 97
Chocolate Sauerkraut Cake, 141
Cultured Muffins, 139
Fruit Compote, 111
Ginger Bug Gingerbread, 137
Live-Fermented Smoothies, 115
prebiotics, 6, 108, 111, 133
probiotics, 5, 12, 14, 16, 24, 75, 99, 111, 113, 145
psychobiotics, 12
Pureed SCOBY, 79
Alive Applesauce, 108
Banana Smash, 109
Fruit Compote, 111
Fruit Leather, 145
Garden Chili, 125

Jun-aigrette, 147
Jun Sourdough Bread, 131–133
Live-Fermented Jam, 113
Live-Fermented Gazpacho, 123
Live-Fermented Smoothies, 115
Raw Pickled Salsa, 117
SCOBY Body Scrub, 155
Tahini Cookies, 143

R
Raw Apple Cider Vinegar, 89. *See also* apple cider vinegar.
raw pickling, 9–25
Raw Pickled Beets, 49. *See also* beets.
Raw Pickled Egg Salad, 127
Raw Pickled Dilly Beans, 51
Raw Pickled Garlic, 39. *See also* garlic.
Raw Pickled Peppers, 41. *See also* peppers.
Raw Pickled Potato Salad, 129. *See also* potatoes.
Raw Pickled Root Vegetables, 55
Raw Pickled Salsa, 117
Raw Pickled Stalks, 61
Raw Pickled Summer Squash/Zucchini, 45
Raw Pickled Watermelon Rind, 65
Raw Pickled Weeds, 63
Raw Pickles, 32–33
Rejuvelac, 105
root vegetables
Raw Pickled Root Vegetables, 55

S
salsa
Raw Pickled Salsa, 117
salad dressing. See *Jun-aigrette*.
sanitization, 22
sauerkraut, 15–16, 19, 23–24, 29
Live-Fermented Sauerkraut, 30–31
Chocolate Sauerkraut Cake, 141
Fermented Facial Mask, 156
Garden Chili, 125
Sauerkraut Focaccia, 135
Sauerruben. See turnips
SCOBY, 17, 75–77, 85

Alive Applesauce, 108
Banana Smash, 109
Fruit Compote, 111
Fruit Leather, 145
Garden Chili, 125
Jun-aigrette, 147
Jun Sourdough Bread, 131–133
Live-Fermented Gazpacho
Live-Fermented Jam, 113
Live-Fermented Smoothies, 115
Pureed SCOBY, 79
Raw Pickled Salsa, 117
SCOBY Body Scrub, 155
SCOBY Doos (Fermented Pet Treats), 151
Tahini Cookies, 143
Second Ferments, 81
Serotonin, 10
Shrub or Switchel, 91
Skinaigrette, 154
Smoothies, 115
Stalks, 61
starter, 14, 17, 24, 75
summer squash
Raw Pickled Summer Squash/Zucchini, 45
superfoods, 5
sweet potatoes
Live-Fermented Sweet Potatoes, 47
Cultured Muffins, 139
Live-Fermented Smoothies, 115
Sweet Potato Fly, 97
Chocolate Sauerkraut Cake, 141
Cultured Muffins, 139
Fruit Compote, 111
Ginger Bug Gingerbread, 137
Live-Fermented Smoothies, 115
Switchel, 91
synbiotic, 6

T
Tahini Cookies, 143
terroir, 2, 85
Tisane. See Cold-Fermented Cooler Tea.
tomatoes, 53
Garden Chili, 125

Live-Fermented Gazpacho, 123
Live-Fermented Tomatoes, 53
Raw Pickled Salsa, 117
Tomato Sauce, 53
Traditional Bread Kvass, 103
turnips, 31, 54, 55, 125, 127, 129, 135, 141
Live-Fermented Turnips: Sauerruben, 54
Garden Chili, 125

V
vagus nerve, 10
vinegar, 9, 13, 17, 23, 77, 83. See also apple
cider vinegar.
viruses, 1, 43

W
watermelon rind
Raw Pickled Watermelon Rind, 65
weeds
Raw Pickled Weeds, 63
wild fermentation, vi, 17

Y
yeast, ix, 1, 17, 23–24, 75, 131–132

Z
zucchini. See summer squash.

ABOUT THE AUTHORS

Susan Crowther writes books on wellness and culinary arts. Susan fell in love with raw pickling while attending a workshop based on Sandor Katz's book, *Wild Fermentation.* Formerly a chef and teacher, she now runs *FerMont,* a fermented farmstand. She lives in Vermont with her husband and dogs.

Julie DuCharme Fallone is an artist who has made food her career and passion from an early age. She has run a restaurant kitchen and a catering company and written a newspaper food column. Today she devotes her time to food photography and jewelry making from her apartment in Baltimore, Maryland.

ABOUT THE CONTRIBUTORS

Donica Krebs, select recipes and photography:

Donica Krebs inherited her love of garden-to-table cooking from her Italian grandparents. She inherited her love of fermentation from a random woman she met in a parking lot (Susan). Donica enjoys foraging and fermentation and resides in East Tennessee with her husband and son on their homestead.

Taylor Hill, foreword and sidebars:

Taylor Hill is a Naturopathic Doctor licensed in Arizona. Currently, he is working on a Doctor of Acupuncture degree and plans to center his future medical practice on Traditional Chinese Medicine. He has presented lectures on the mind-gut connection and its wide-reaching effects on human health. He also helped start a business teaching others how to make fermented foods. Taylor started fermenting in 2014 when he got his first SCOBY. He lives in Mesa, Arizona, with his two children.

ACKNOWLEDGMENTS

Warm thanks extend to the following:

To the incomparable Julie D. Fallone: food photographer, visual author, and recipe developer. Julie has my back in all our book projects, and this one in particular. For carrying me through the hardest year of my life (that's another story), I am eternally grateful. To Donica, a kindred spirit and fellow fermenting wacko. I look forward to future collaborations with you and Julie, and also to handing over the baton. You already got this. Thanks to Taylor Hill for his sidebar contributions and enthusiasm. Thank you, Brian Mooney, for the literary giggles and sardonic encouragement. Thanks to the Whetstone Ledges Farm ladies, Gail MacArthur and Lauren Beigel MacArthur, for allowing me to experiment with fermented goodies. To Steven Gruber, badass chiropractor, for keeping my "edit neck" in good form. Deep gratitude extends to Abigail Gehring Lawrence for her enduring publishing support, and to the Skyhorse family, for giving me opportunities to share my passions. And always, to my husband Markos, thank you for your constancy in love, laughter, and foot rubs. Beso.

—Susan Crowther